ACPL, Laramie, WY   6/2018
39102100002483
Aye, Nila
Drawing school /
Pieces:1

WITHDRAWN

D0520764

DRAWING SCHOOL

Illustrated by Nila Aye

Albany County
Public Library
Laramie, Wyoming

Table of Contents

Welcome to Drawing School!

Get your pencils sharpened, your erasers ready, and your artist's hat on—it's time to draw!

Tools & Materials

Pencils

Whether you like a regular pencil or a fancy mechanical one, it doesn't really matter. Just remember to sketch lightly at first, so it's easier to erase. You can always darken your lines later!

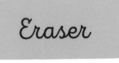

Eraser

It's a good idea to have a quality eraser on hand, not just the one on the end of your pencil! Just in case you draw any lines you want to change.

Ruler
When you need to make super straight lines, a small ruler works like a charm.

Paper
You can doodle on anything you'd like: a notebook, copy paper, scratch paper…whatever strikes your fancy! But if you're making a drawing you want to keep around for awhile, use some heavier, nicer drawing paper you can get at any arts and crafts store.

Color
Colored pencils, markers, crayons, paints—they're all great! Choose what works best for you.

Seeing Shapes

The easiest way to learn how to draw is to look for the shapes and lines that make up what you're trying to draw.

Some shapes are easy to see:

And some take a little more thought:

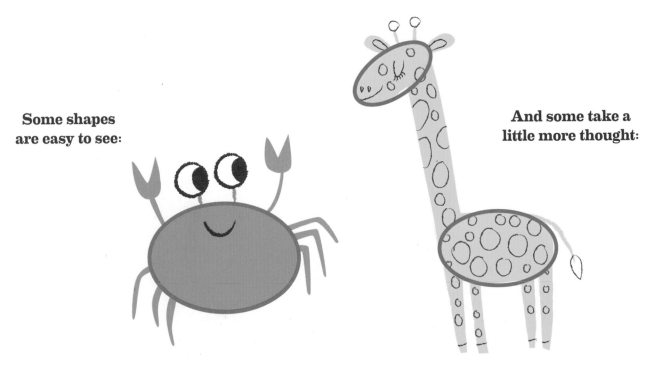

These are some shapes you should get to know, so you can recognize them easily when you're drawing!

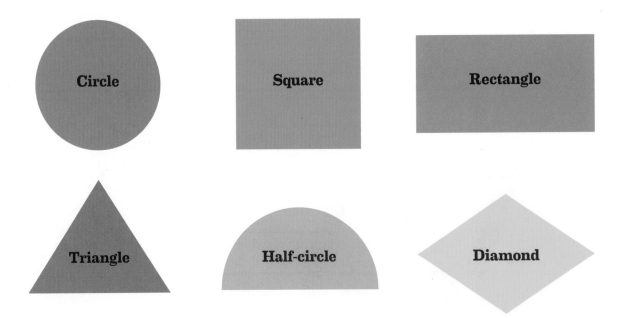

Circle

Square

Rectangle

Triangle

Half-circle

Diamond

Sometimes you'll see other shapes too, like these:

jelly bean shape

"M" shape

What shapes do you see?

Learning Lines

The lines we draw are just as important as the shapes we use.

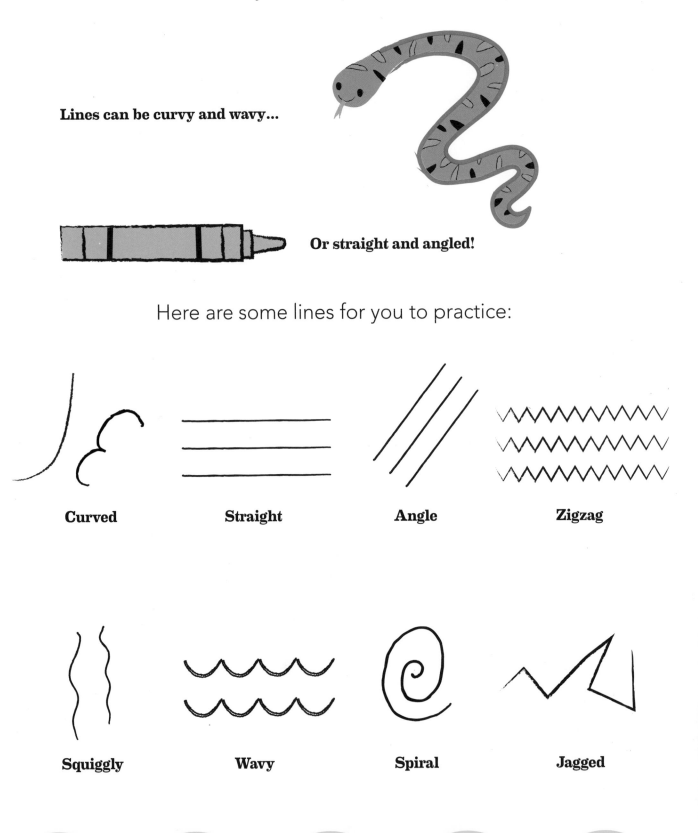

Lines can be curvy and wavy...

Or straight and angled!

Here are some lines for you to practice:

Curved   **Straight**   **Angle**   **Zigzag**

Squiggly   **Wavy**   **Spiral**   **Jagged**

Sometimes it's easier to start a drawing with
an outline of the shape you're trying to draw, like this:

What lines do you see?

Pets

goldfish

Begin with an oval and a curved line for the bowl.

canary

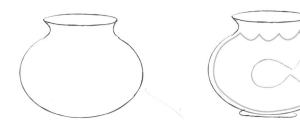

Draw a half circle for the head, then add another half circle for the body.

Meow! Woof! Squawk! Your favorite furry, feathered, and scaly companions make great subjects for drawing. Start with a few basic shapes and simple lines, and you can draw dapper dogs, cuddly kittens, brilliant birds, and even leaping lizards!

Then add simple shapes for your fish, and fill in the water too.

Fill in a bright yellow, and then add all the details.

cat

First draw an oval for the head and add the eyes, ears, and face.

sleeping kitten

Use a circle for the head and triangles for the ears.

cuddly kitten

All you need is an oval to start, then add triangle ears and circle eyes.

Draw the body and add long, thin ovals for the legs, and a tail!

Then add its curved body and cute, itty bitty paws.

A long, thin oval for the body and smaller ovals for the legs and tail. Meow!

13

dog

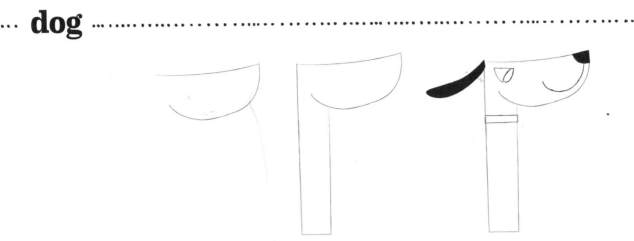

Begin with a half circle that's not quite closed, and add a rectangle body.

playful puppy

This cute puppy starts with a oval shape with a pointed end for his nose,
then a teardrop shape for his ear.

begging puppy

Start with a round shape for the head and a triangle shape for the ear.

Once you've got that in place, just add legs, spots, and a tail.

Add his legs and wagging tail, and he's ready to play!

Add ovals for the body and paws, then add his hind legs and tail.

lizard

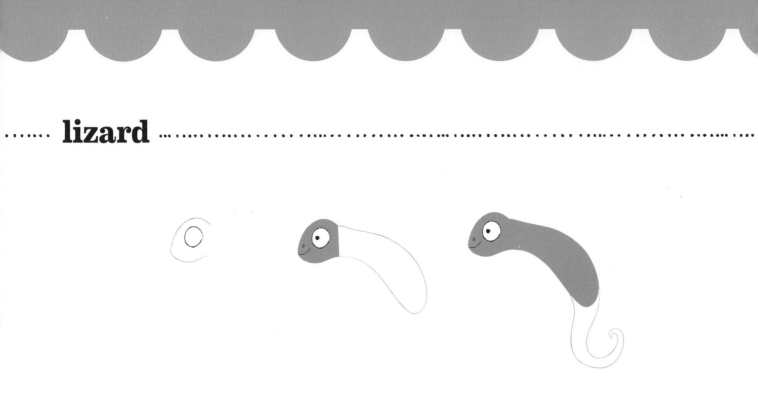

This little guy is all curved lines! Use a spiral for his tail, almost like a fish hook.

turtle

The turtle's shell is like a half circle, with a slightly pointed end
at the front where his head comes out.

Use a bright color for him, so he really stands out!

Add rectangles for legs and a cool circle pattern on his shell.

parrot

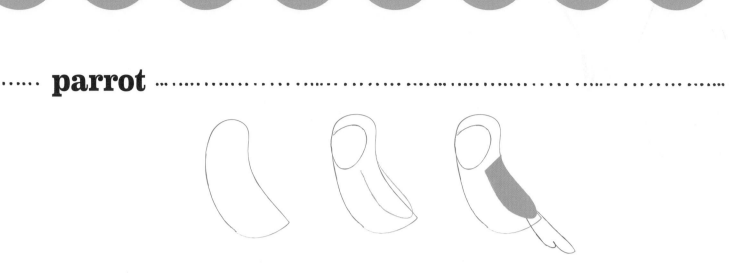

This colorful parrot is made of curved lines, plus a circle for the face.

snake

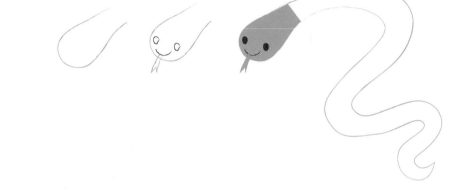

A snake is all curvy lines! Start with the head, and then add the curvy body.

spider

This fun little creepy crawler is an easy doodle to do! Start with some circles.

Add the details and be sure to use bright colors for the feathers.

Fill in the main color, and then add a fun pattern.

Add curved lines for legs and dots for feet. Now draw her strand of silk!

bunny

Once you have the circles for the face in place, add the bunny's ears.

hamster in a wheel

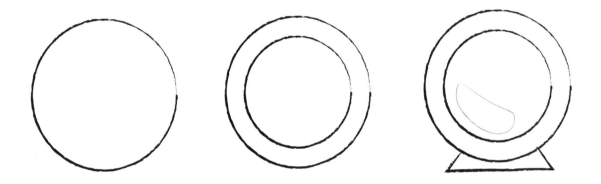

Draw one circle inside of another. Then add the base and an oval for the hamster's body.

Then draw a big oval for the body and add the paws. Don't forget a fluffy tail!

Add the details on your hamster, then add the detail lines for his spinning wheel.

dog bone

 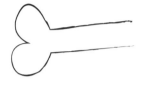 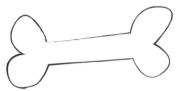

A dog bone is really just two straight lines with a couple
of curved lines at each end, almost like hearts.

bird cage

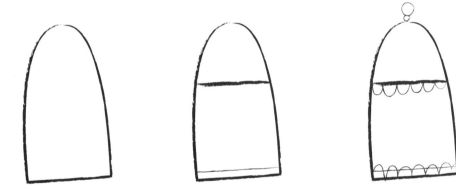

Start with half an oval, and add straight and curved lines inside for detail.

dog bowl

Begin with an oval. Then add two straight lines for the sides and a curved line for the bottom. Add a lighter color for the inside of the bowl, and one more curved line to show the bottom.

Add more details to the cage, and some curved lines for the top and feet.

24

25

Sports Stuff

····· **soccer player** ···

Start with a circle for the player's head, and then add a skinny triangle for his body.

····· **soccer ball** ···

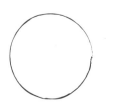 

For the pattern on a soccer ball, start with a pentagon shape—which just means it has five sides.

What's your favorite sport? Whether you like to ski through snowy mountains or chase a ball across the field, you can learn to draw it all! From race car drivers to ice skaters, all you need are some simple shapes and lines to doodle the sports and athletes that catch your eye. Go team!

Add rectangles for arms and legs, and put some spikes on those cleats!

Add a few more partial pentagons, and then connect them all together.

football player

For the helmet, start with a curved line, and then add two straight lines.
Add squares for the face and body.

football

Draw a curved line like a smile, then add an upside-down smile on top of it.

cheerleader

A simple circle for her head, then add her pigtails, body, and the fluffy shapes of her pompoms.

Add the arms and legs, and use your team's colors for the uniform.

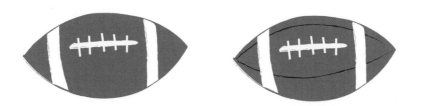

Add the details and you're ready for the game!

Add some color and the details. Let's go, team!

basketball

Start with an orange circle and two curved lines.

basketball player

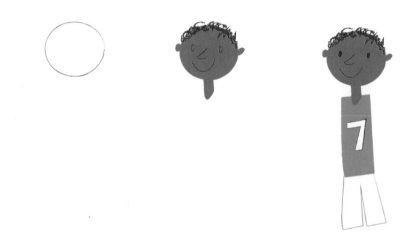

Once you've got his head and neck in place, add rectangles for his body.

gymnast

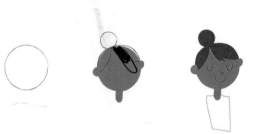

Start with a simple set of circles. Add her face and a rectangle for her body.

Add one curved line down the center, and one from side to side. Slam dunk!

Then draw his arms with skinny rectangles and add a spinning ball for a finishing touch!

Then draw her graceful arms and legs with long, curved lines.

baseball player

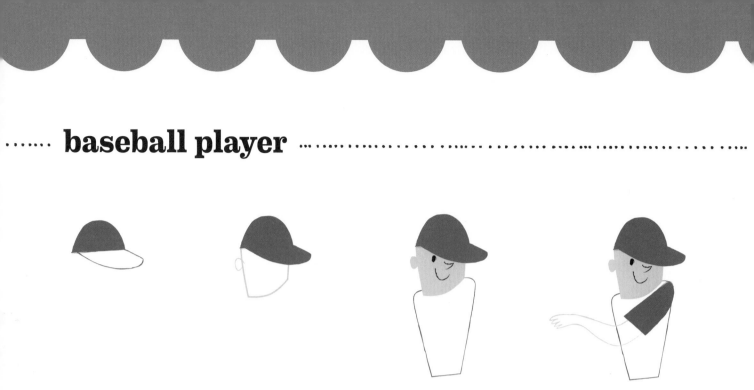

Two half-circles make the hat. Then add rectangles for his body and curvy lines for his arm.

race car with driver

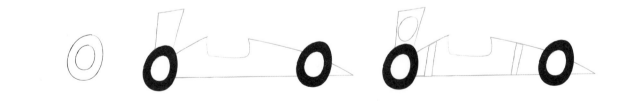

Build this car from the wheels up! Use rectangles and triangles for the car.

Draw his legs, then add the details and a bat. Swing, batter, swing!

Add the driver with a C-shape for his head and an L-shape for his arms.

33

ice skate

Begin with half of a rectangle, then add the curved bottom of the skate.

ice skater

Her head is all circles and curved lines! Add ovals for her arms and a pointy oval for her skirt.

skier

Begin with a circle for his head and a triangle for his hat.
Then draw his arms with an "L" shape and a rectangle.

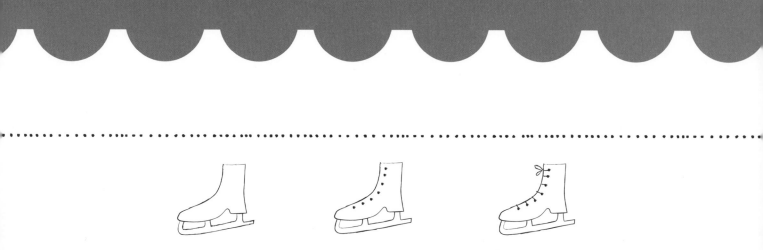

Add the blade, and then the laces.

Long ovals for legs and a pair of skates, and she's ready to twirl!

Give him a scarf, mittens, and skis and poles, of course!

Let's Celebrate

····· **cupcake** ··

Start with three straight lines and a spiky top for the base. Then add the cupcake.

····· **birthday cake** ···

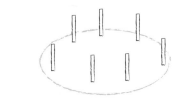 

A birthday cake is made of an oval and a few straight lines too!

Any day is a good day for a party! Cake, balloons, presents...they're all here. There's even a colorful piñata to swing a stick at. Come on, let's party!

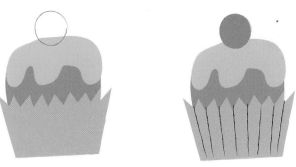

After putting some fluffy frosting on top, don't forget to add the cherry!

Decorate however you like, and make a wish!

balloons

Start with a circle. Add a triangle at the bottom, and a curvy line for the string.

gift

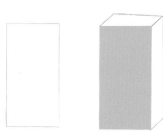   

Begin with a rectangle, then add the sides. Draw a pretty bow on top too!

piñata

Stack two rectangles on top of each other. Then add triangles for the face and ears.

Balloons come in many shapes and colors. Get creative!

Or keep it simple with a rectangle and a few lines.

Use lots of bright colors to fill in your shapes, and squiggly lines to show the texture.

On the Farm

cow

Start with a small rectangle for the head and a bigger one for the body. Then add the face and horns.

horse

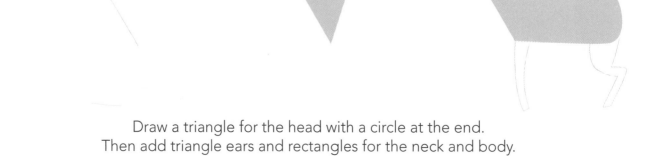

Draw a triangle for the head with a circle at the end.
Then add triangle ears and rectangles for the neck and body.

44

Mooooo. Oink. Baaaah. There's so much to draw on the farm! You can draw a crowing rooster, a rumbling tractor, and a big red barn. The sun is shining, the pigs are rolling in the mud, and the cat's asleep in the hay. Let's get drawing on the farm!

Add the udder, legs, and tail. Color her in, and don't forget to leave room for some spots!

Finish off by drawing the legs, mane, and tail. Giddyup!

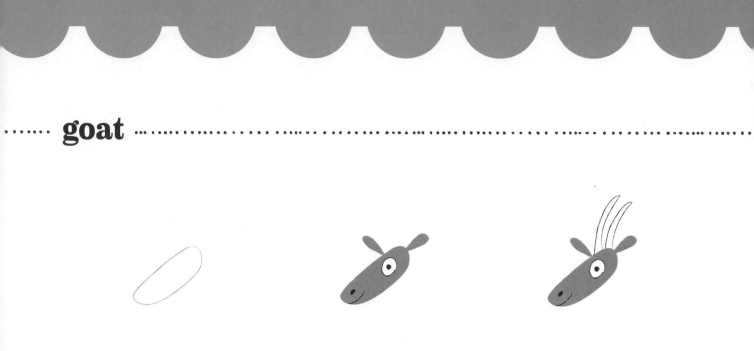

goat

This hairy goat starts with a simple oval for his head and a circle for his eye.
Then add his ears and horns.

sheep

Start with a squiggly cloud shape. Then add a "U" shape for the sheep's face.

Add a few angled lines for his body.
Use short, curved lines to show his furry belly, and little "U" shapes for his feet.

Draw another big fluffy cloud shape for her body, and draw her legs and tail too.

duck

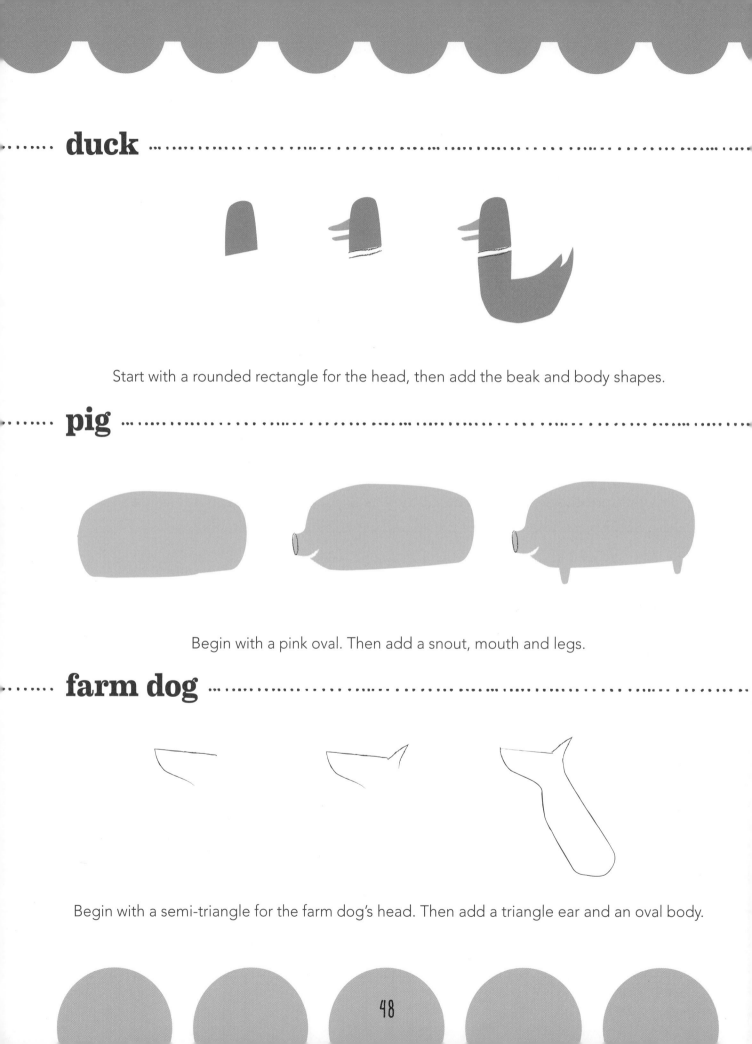

Start with a rounded rectangle for the head, then add the beak and body shapes.

pig

Begin with a pink oval. Then add a snout, mouth and legs.

farm dog

Begin with a semi-triangle for the farm dog's head. Then add a triangle ear and an oval body.

Then add the feet, eye and wing.

Add the ear and the other two legs. Finish up with an eye, another ear, and a cute curly tail.

Add his legs and tail, and his friendly face. Awww, it looks like he wants a treat!

hen

Start with an oval shape for the head, and use a half-circle shape for the body and tail.

chick

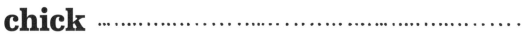

The chick's body is an oval with a little tiny triangle at the end. Add a circle for the eye.

rooster

Draw a circle for the head, then make a ruffled bottom and add the eye.
Use curved lines for the body and feathers.

Add the feet, beak, and comb and wattle (the red parts). Use a "U" shape for the eye.

Two tiny triangles make the beak, and three lines make each leg.

Add the legs, beak, and comb and wattle. Cock-a-doodle-doo!

scarecrow

Use a half-circle for the hat, and another for the face. Add rectangles for the body and arms.

corn

Use a long skinny, oval to start, then use curved and angled lines for the leaves.

crow

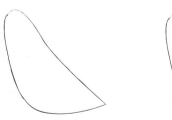  

Start with a rounded shape for the crow's body, and use curved lines for the wing.

More rectangles for the legs, and the patches on the shirt too!

Draw a grid of slightly curved lines to show all the kernels.

Fill it in with black, and add feet and a yellow beak!

farmer

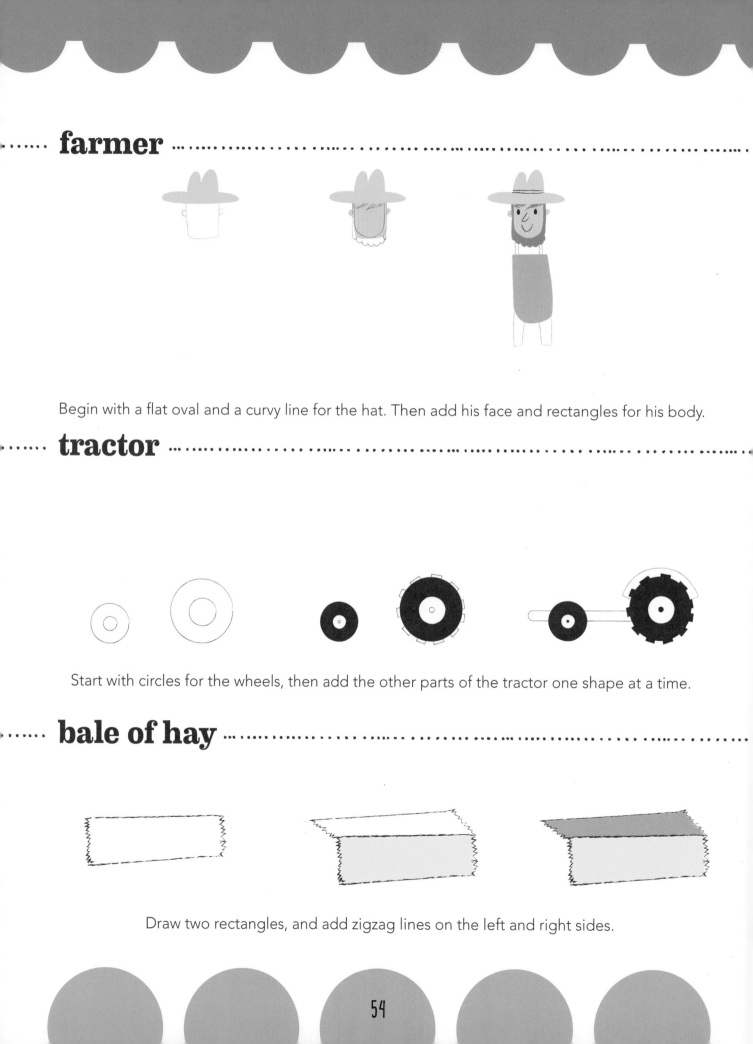

Begin with a flat oval and a curvy line for the hat. Then add his face and rectangles for his body.

tractor

Start with circles for the wheels, then add the other parts of the tractor one shape at a time.

bale of hay

Draw two rectangles, and add zigzag lines on the left and right sides.

Draw his arms and boots, and don't forget his pitchfork and pail!

Add the tread on the tires and the steering wheel, and color the tractor a bright red.

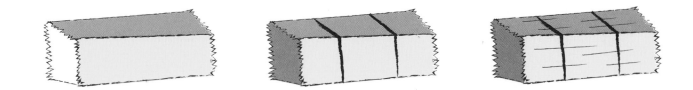

Use more zigzags to show the texture of the hay, and add straight lines for the binding.

sunflower

Draw a brown circle for the center, then fill in around it with yellow oval petals.

farm cat

Start with ovals for the head and body, and triangle ears.

mouse

Use curved lines for the outline of the body, and draw big ears and tiny feet.

Add another color of petal behind the yellow ones, and then draw a green stem and leaves.

Use curved lines for the cat's tail, and add little triangles for stripes.

Add a nose, whiskers, and tail, and maybe even a tiny piece of cheese!

 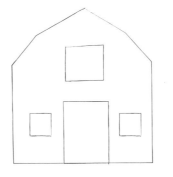 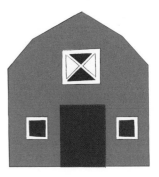

Start with a simple rectangle. Then add a triangle roof and squares for the windows.

farmhouse

  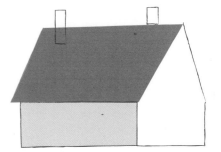

The roof looks like a slanted rectangle.
Once you have the roof, add straight lines to draw the rest of the house.

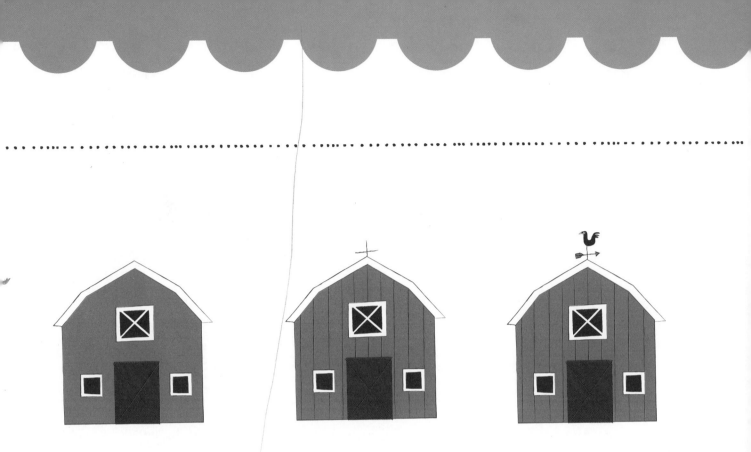

Add all the details, including the weather vane on top, and then paint your barn bright red!

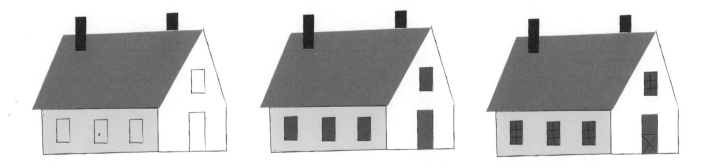

Add the windows, doors, and chimneys, and you've got a farmhouse!

61

At the Beach

sailboat

Use straight lines to draw the shape of the boat, and add circles for the portholes.

beach umbrella

Begin with a half-circle, and add two curved lines for the stripes.

Sunny days are here again at the beach! Sailboats and bikinis, palm trees and sand castles—they're all here on the sandy shores. Get your shades ready. Let's draw a day at the beach!

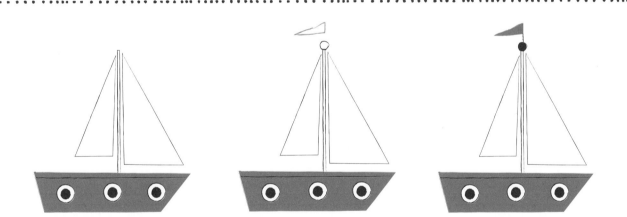

Add a mast and triangles for the sails. Ahoy, mate!

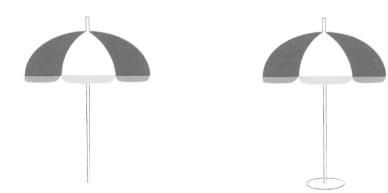

Fill in the colors and add the stand. Now you've got some cool shade!

sun

This friendly sun begins with a big yellow circle.
Add two circles for the eyes and curved lines to finish the eyes and smile.

waves

To show movement in water, like waves, just add some "wavy" lines!
Start with a "U" shape, and then connect it to two or three others.

palm tree

Start with a spidery shape, using long, curved lines for the palm leaves.

Now add triangles for the rays of the sun, and color it all in. Shine on!

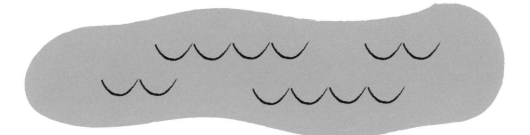

Vary the length and number of waves you make, so it looks like a real ocean shore.

Draw a long, thin trunk, and then add the details on the trunk.

beach ball

Begin with a large circle, and draw a straight line right down the middle.

bikini

Draw two triangles for the top, then add a thin rectangle and curved lines for the bottom.

sunglasses

These cool shades are really just two half-circles with some straight lines.

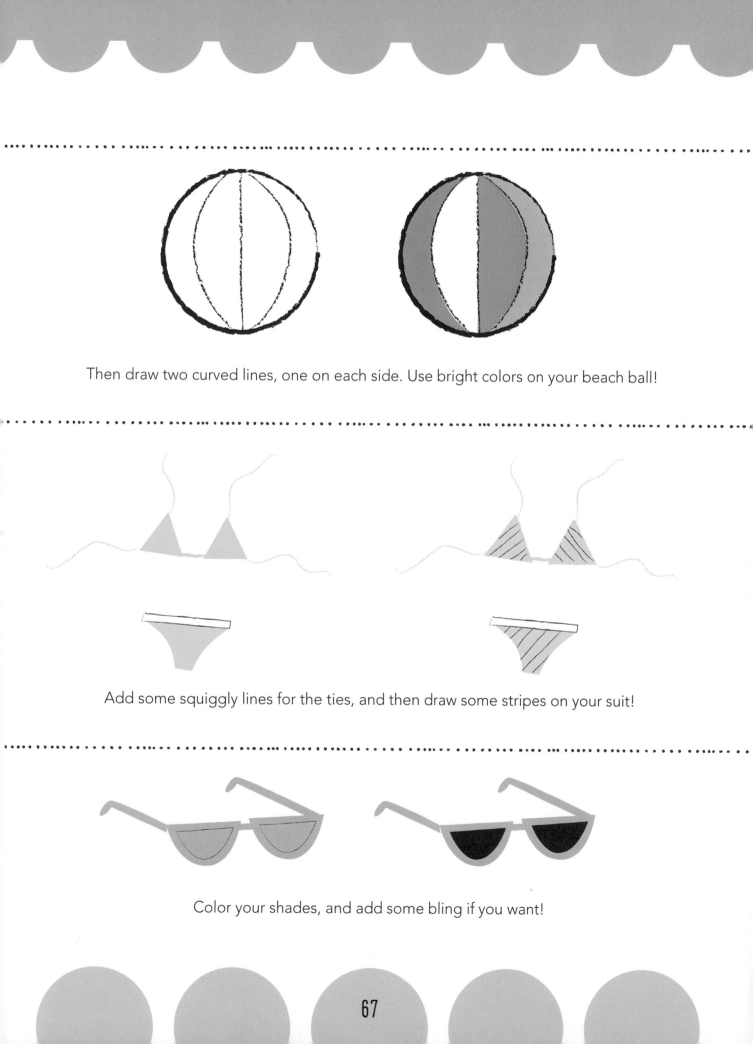

Then draw two curved lines, one on each side. Use bright colors on your beach ball!

Add some squiggly lines for the ties, and then draw some stripes on your suit!

Color your shades, and add some bling if you want!

sand castle

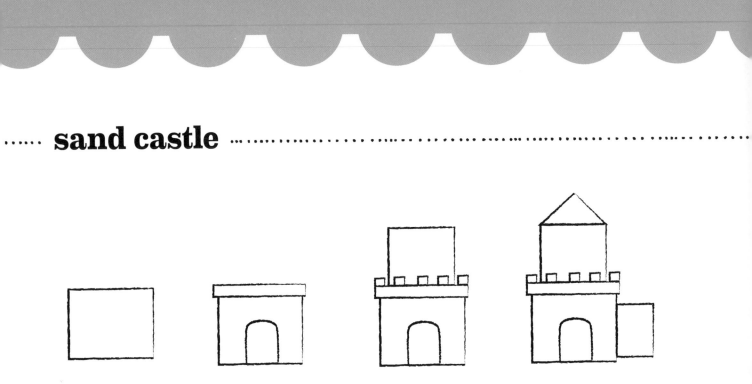

Build this sand castle with rectangles. Start with a base, and add the door and tiny squares on top.

pail

For the pail, start with an oval at the top, then draw a curved line
for the bottom and connect it with straight lines.

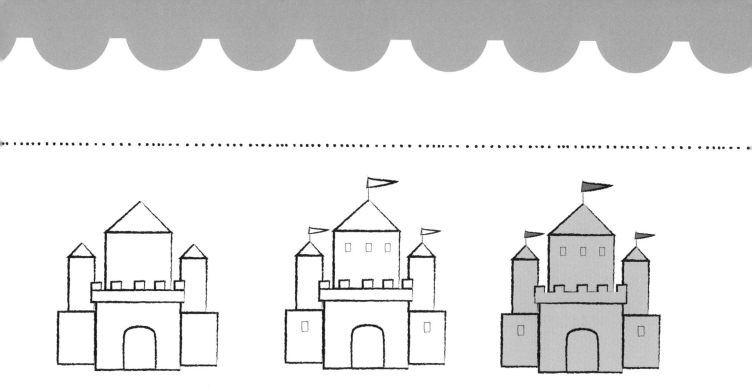

Then add the rest of the castle, using more rectangles and triangles for the tops.

shovel

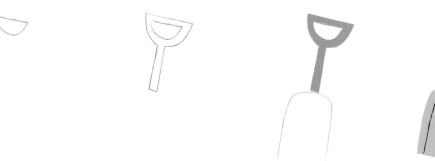

For the shovel, begin with a half-circle, and then draw the handle around it.
Draw two upside-down "U" shapes for the bottom.

round seashell

This shell is like a big half-circle with a little triangle at the bottom.

spiral seashell

Start with a circle, then draw a rounded triangle shape on the right side.

anchor

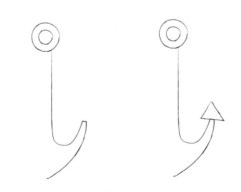

Begin with a small circle within a circle. Then use curved lines to draw one side of the anchor, and add a triangle tip.

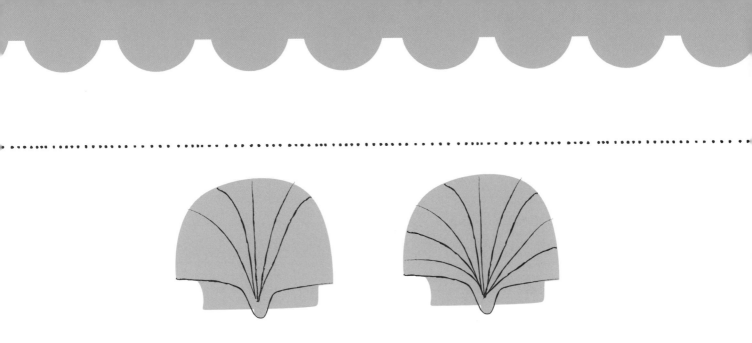

Add a rectangle to fill out the bottom, and then draw the details.

Now add the spiral in the center of the shell.

Now fill in the other side, and add a rectangle near the top and rope around the anchor.

lighthouse

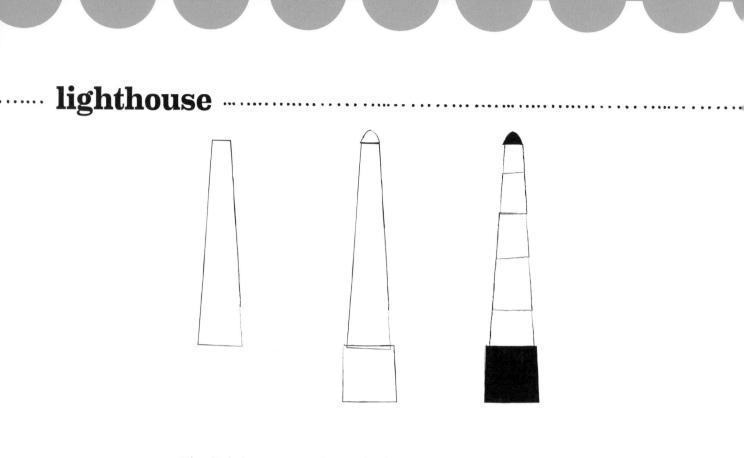

The lighthouse is wider at the bottom than it is at the top,
so your straight lines need to point slightly toward each other.

sailor

Let's start with the sailor's hat! Once you have that in place, add his face and shirt.

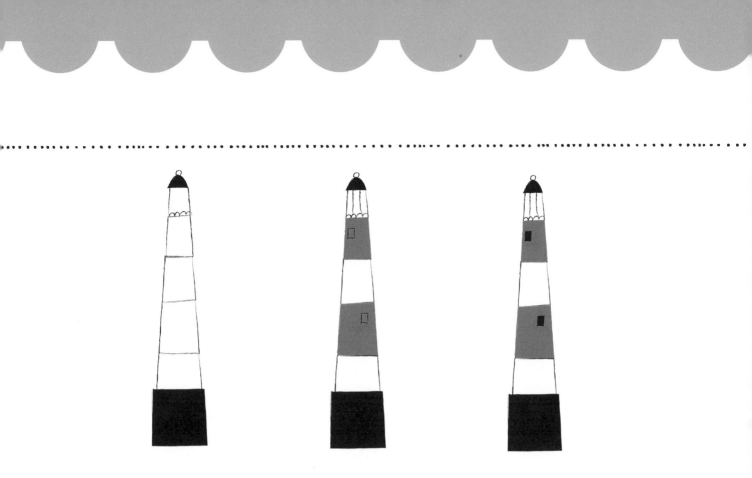

Add a square base, a triangle top, and some bright stripes to your lighthouse.

Then draw his wide-legged pants and give him some shoes too. Ready to set sail?

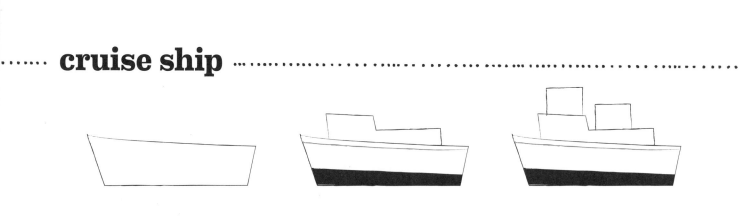

cruise ship

Draw a rectangle that is a little taller on one side. Then add the shapes for the rest.

tourist

Start with a circle for the head and add a half-circle for his hat.
Then draw his face and add his colorful shirt.

camera

Draw a rectangle first, then add the details with smaller circles and rectangles.

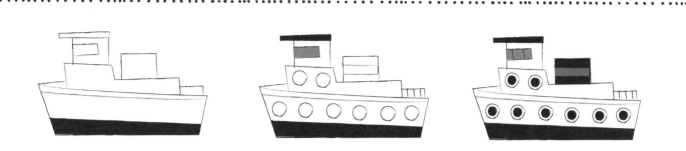

Add stripes, circles for the windows, and all the other details!

He needs bright shorts, and socks with sandals, of course! Don't forget to add his fanny pack.

Add the final details, and this camera is ready to capture your day at the beach!

Under the Sea

yellow fish

Start with a yellow triangle for the body. Add its fins, mouth, and tail next.

pink tropical fish

This colorful fish's body is a circle with a triangle at the end.

78

The ocean is filled with cool creatures that are very different from what we see on land! Explore it by drawing different sea animals, like tropical fish, mighty whales, puffy puffer fish, and friendly dolphins. You might even find some sunken treasure!

Now add the rest of the details: the eye, green fins, and stripes.

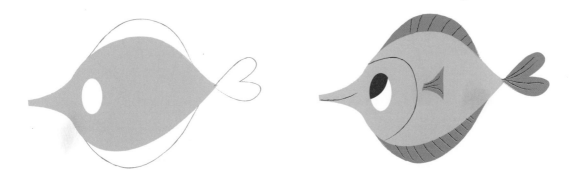

Draw curved lines for the fins, and add a heart-shaped tail. Then finish off the details!

scuba diver

Use ovals for the face and mask, and curvy pointed lines for the hair. Then add the curved body.

coral

Coral looks like a willowy underwater tree. Start by lightly sketching the base, then add curved lines for the branches.

seaweed

Waving in the water, seaweed is all curvy lines!
Start with one line in the middle, and build out from there.

The fins are just two curvy triangles. Add a rectangle for the oxygen tank too!

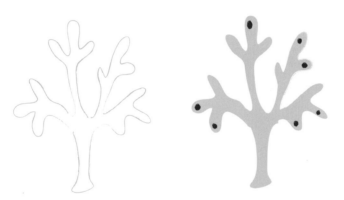

Fill in with color, and add some tiny dots for details.

Once the lines are in place, add tiny straight lines to show all the leaves.

jellyfish

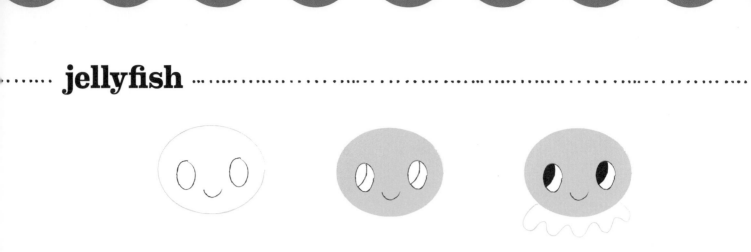

This friendly fellow starts with a smiley face inside an oval!

dolphin

Begin with a rounded triangle shape for the body.
Then add curvy triangles for the fin, flipper, and tail, and an oval for the eye.

Add some curvy lines for the rest of his body, and some long, curved lines for his tentacles.

Use two small round shapes for the mouth and a tiny circle
for the blowhole on top of her head!

sea lion

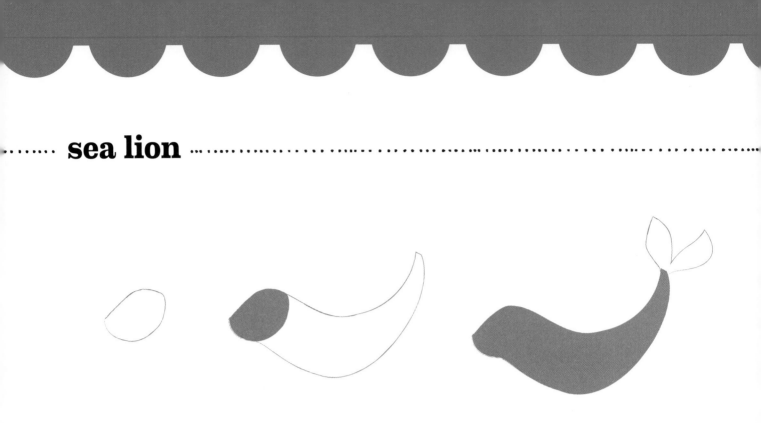

For this sweet sea lion, draw an oval shape for the head first.
Then add the long, tapering body and two flowy triangle shapes for the back flippers.

crab

This funny crab is all circles and skinny legs! Start with his body and eyes.

84

Of the two front flippers, the one that's closest to you should look a little bigger.
Give her some whiskers too!

Then draw his legs. Don't forget the claws!

lobster

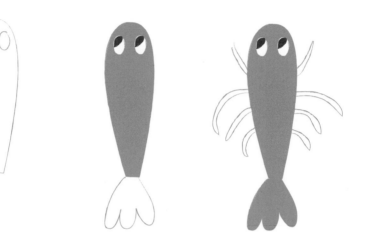

Give this lobster six legs and two big front claws.

octopus

Begin with a rounded rectangle for the body.
Then draw her face, and add four of her curvy tentacles.

Use long, curved lines for its antennae, and some smaller detail lines to show the sections of the shell.

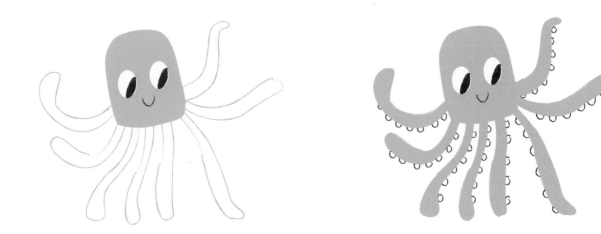

Add four more tentacles, and then draw little semi-circle suckers on each of her tentacles.

shark

Start with two curved lines for the body, like a crescent moon shape.
Then add his eye and fin, and the bottom half of his body.

treasure chest

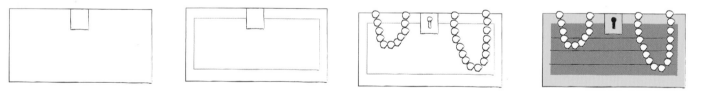

Draw a rectangle first, and add a smaller rectangle inside and a square for the lock.
Draw small circles for the pearls and trim too.

Use triangles for his other fin and tail, then draw in his gills and teeth.
He looks too happy to bite!

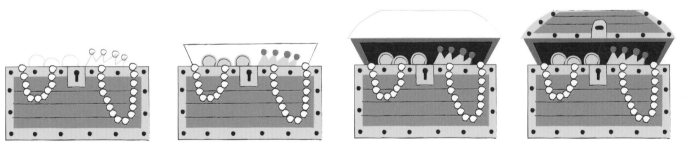

Then add the lid and more treasure inside. Happy treasure hunting!

sea turtle

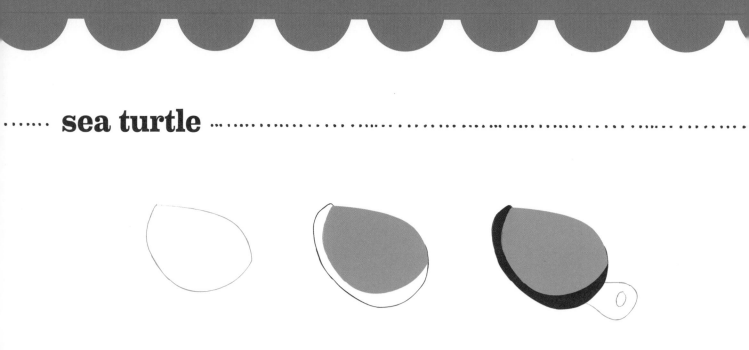

The turtle's shell is an oval with a pointed end, and his head is a small oval.

whale

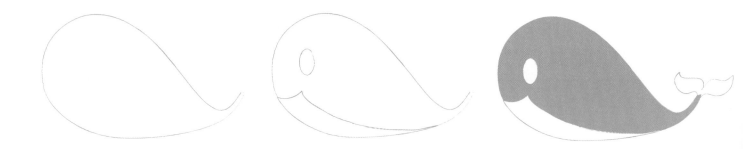

This whale's body looks like a giant raindrop on its side, doesn't it?

Add curvy triangle shapes for his flippers, and then draw the pattern on his shell and body.

Use curved lines for her tail, her belly, and the spout of water at the top too!

seahorse

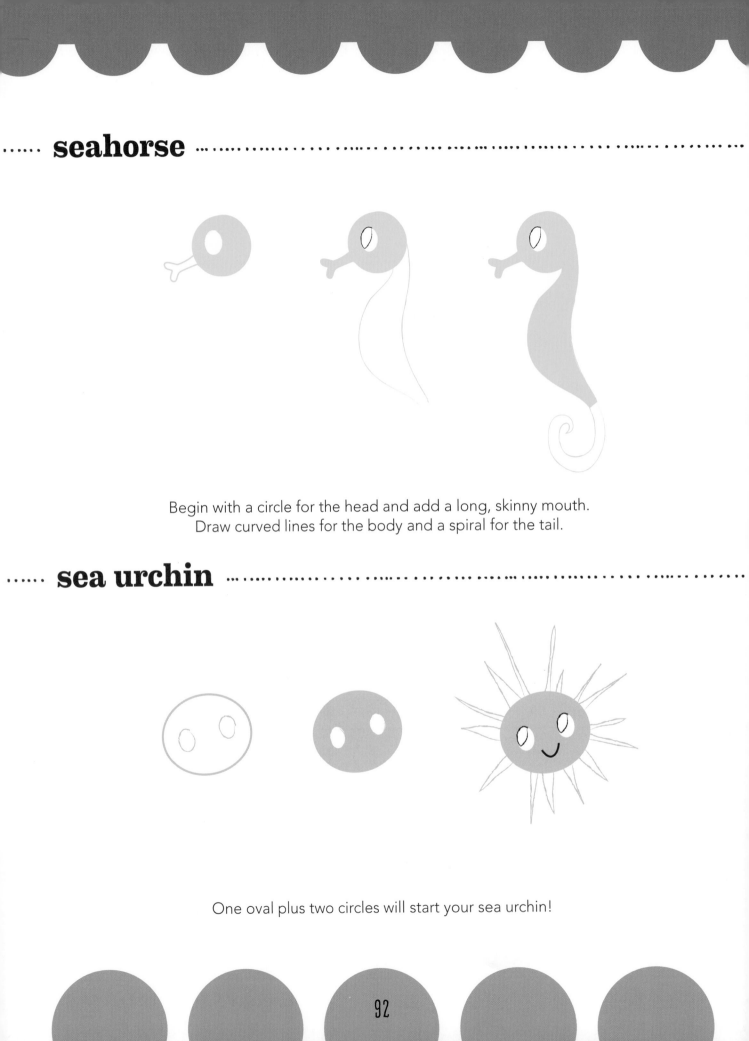

Begin with a circle for the head and add a long, skinny mouth.
Draw curved lines for the body and a spiral for the tail.

sea urchin

One oval plus two circles will start your sea urchin!

Fill it all in, and add a triangle fin. Draw a spiky spine down the back,
and then give her some stripes—and eyelashes!

Then add some spikes of all different sizes to show off its prickly powers.

sea star

Start this simple star with the first two sides of a triangle.
Then add four more of the same!

stingray

Two curved lines make a giant smiley shape. Add a curved line
for the head and draw the rest of the body.

puffer fish

Draw a big circle to start, then add a face and a triangle fin.

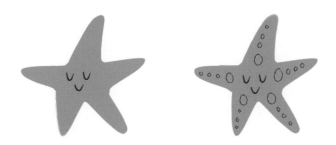

Tiny circles show off this super starfish's suckers.

Use curvy lines for the tail, and add all the final details too.

Use round lines for the face, but short, small triangle shapes for the puffer's spikes.

95

At the Zoo

zookeeper

Begin with a circle for her head, then add her hat and body.

gorilla

The gorilla's face is an oval shape with two curvy sides.
Draw his body with a curved oval shape too.

Lions, tigers, and bears, oh my! There is so much to see at the zoo, from cuddly koalas and grumpy gorillas to happy hippos and zippy zebras. Grab your drawing gear, and let's go explore a day at the zoo!

Draw her arms, legs and feet, and then draw her pail and all the details on her outfit.

Next add his front and back legs, and color him in all black.

lion

Start with a circle for the lion's head, and then add his shaggy mane with jagged lines around his face.

tiger

Draw a circle for the head, and half-circles for the ears. Add a rectangle body too.

Draw his body with a rectangle, and add four smaller rectangles for his legs. Roar!

Then add the front and back legs, and a long tail. And the stripes, of course!

Draw a circle head on top of a long, curved neck. Add a curved triangle for the beak.

toucan

The colorful toucan has a big green circle around her eye, and a yellow and black body.

Flamingos have very long, thin legs—and pink feet too!

Be sure to give her a full tail and fluffy feathered wings!

penguin

If you start with the penguin's face and beak, the rest of his outline is pretty easy.

polar bear

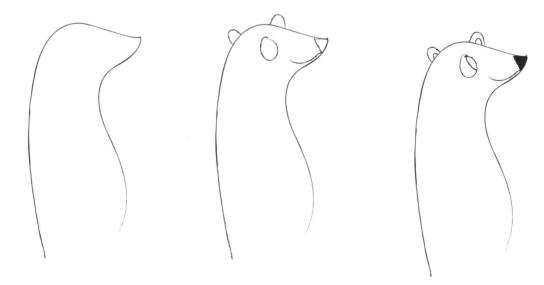

Two curved lines and a pointed nose for the polar bear's snout are all you need to begin.

Be sure to give him orange feet and a black "tuxedo" to complete his look.

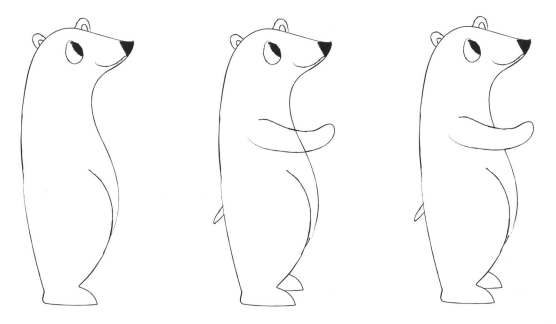

Draw the hind legs, and then add the front arm, reaching forward. More fish, please?

monkey

There's more than one way to make a monkey, but here you can start with the head first, and then add the curved lines of the body.

rhino

The rhino's body looks like a big jelly bean!
Draw a rectangle shape for the snout and small rectangles for the back legs.

Add a spiraled tail and a curvy front arm too!

Draw the ears, tail, and horns too, and then add the final touches.

zebra

Begin with an outline of the zebra's body, and then add the front and back legs.

camel

Draw the head first, and then the body with a big wavy line to show off the two humps.

Next add the mane and tail, and then add in all those crazy stripes!

Add some long, thin legs, a skinny little tail, and some long eyelashes!

kangaroo

Once you draw the head, add a long pear shape for the body, then draw the tail.

koala

What a cuddly animal! Start with an oval for the koala's head and add long, fringy ears.

elephant

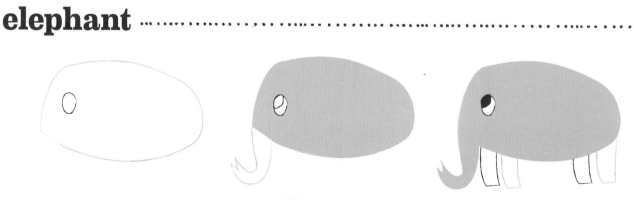

Begin with a big oval for the body, then add the elephant's trunk and legs.

Draw the front and back legs, and don't forget the pocket so this kangaroo can carry her joey!

Since this koala is hugging a tree, draw curved arms and legs so he can hold on tightly.

Elephants have big ears! Whoa, Elly!

111

hippo

This pink hippo starts with a rectangle body and a round head.

giraffe

Giraffes are known for their long, skinny necks! Give yours some tall legs too.

Add legs, ears, and tail, and give her some teeth too!

Now add plenty of brown spots fit for a gorgeous giraffe.

crocodile

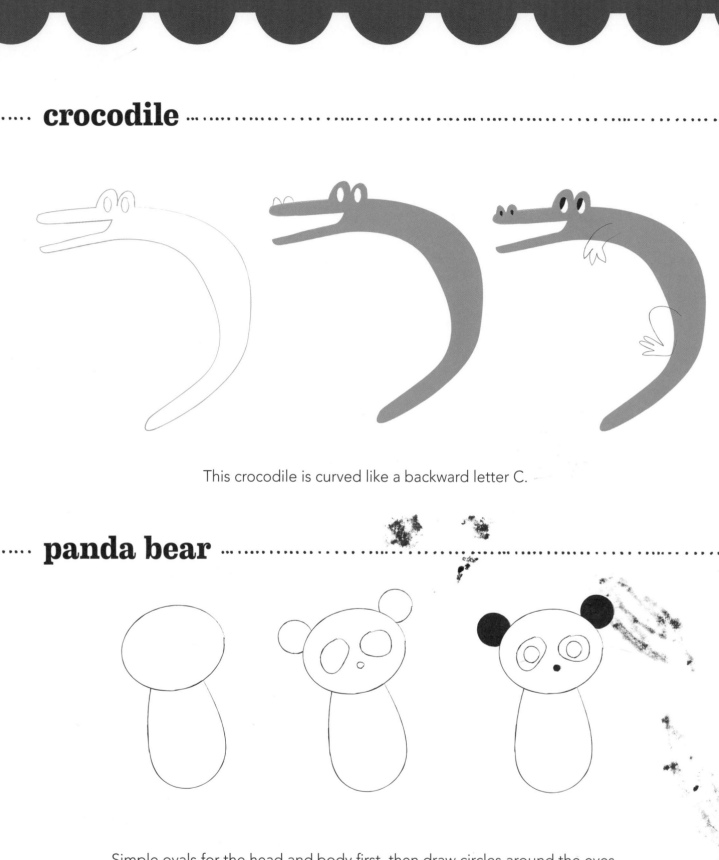

This crocodile is curved like a backward letter C.

panda bear

Simple ovals for the head and body first, then draw circles around the eyes.

Draw spiky spines along his back, and a few sharp teeth too.

Draw arms and legs, and that cute panda bear smile!

117

In the Garden

lovely butterfly

Start with a brown tapered oval for the body, then add the wings.

pretty butterfly

This butterfly is seen from the side, so just draw one set of wings!

How green is your garden? Here among the colorful flowers, buzzing insects, and rows of vegetables, there's a whole world to draw! Befriend a jolly garden gnome, get to know a friendly frog, and see what's blooming today as you learn to draw everything that grows and lives in the garden!

Draw a fun pattern on the wings, and add the final details!

Add a pretty pattern, and some antennae too.

rose

Start with the three largest petals in front. Then add half an oval,
the back petals, and a spiral in the center.

marigold

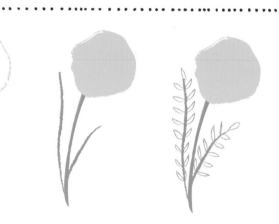

Use a wavy circle for the flower, and draw a long green stem.

pansy

Draw a yellow center, then add purple petals with wavy edges.

Draw a thick stem with thorns, and then fill in your rose with a bright color.

Add the leaves, and tiny wavy lines to show all the little petals.

Then add three small heart shapes at the center, and a stem and leaves.

daffodil

Begin with a wavy oval for the center, and a half-oval for the tubular part of the flower.
Then add the petals one at a time.

bee

Draw a yellow oval, and then add two blue ovals that look like bunny ears.

Draw the stem and one large leaf, and the inside of the daffodil.

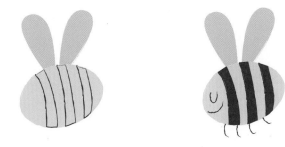

Add the bee's black stripes, four little legs, and a smile!

watering can

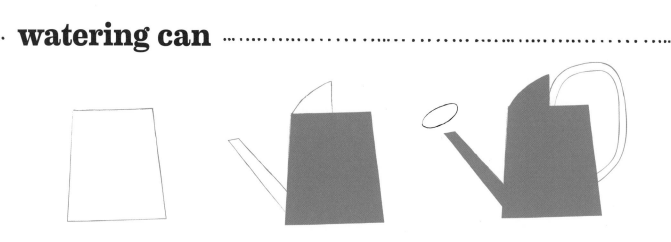

Draw a rectangle that is slightly narrower at the top than the bottom. Add the spout and handle.

gardening gloves

Start with three straight lines at the bottom. Then add the two end fingers.

rain boots

Begin with a thin oval for the top of the boot, then draw two straight lines down from the sides.

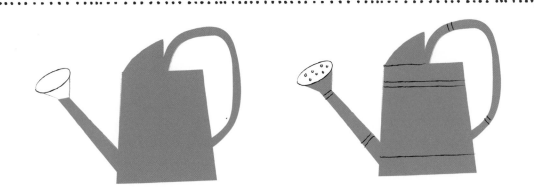

Now add the tip of the spout with an oval and two straight lines. Finish it off!

Fill in the other three fingers, and use a bright color to fill it in!

Draw the curved toe, and add a small square heel at the back. Add the final details.

carrot

Draw a long, skinny triangle, pointing down. Then add a scraggly top, and detail lines to finish.

rabbit

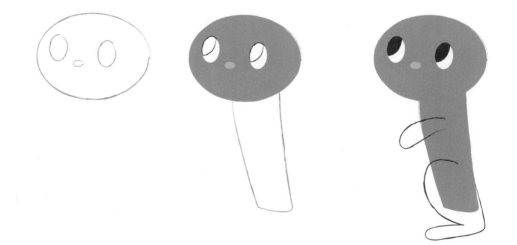

Draw an oval for the head, and a long thin rectangle for the body.

tomato

Draw the stem first, then the spiky top of the tomato. Then add a big red circle!

Add the front and back legs, and two long, floppy ears. Hippity hop!

garden gnome

Draw a big red triangle for the hat and a half-circle for his face.
Add some pointy ears and bushy eyebrows.

mushroom

A half-circle makes the top of the mushroom, and a curvy rectangle shape makes the stem.

Draw in his beard, then add his body. Draw his boots—and buttons too!

Add some big, fun polka dots to the top of the mushroom, and a wavy line to the stem.

frog

Start with two half ovals that look like the letter "M." Add two circles for eyes and a big circle for the body

radish

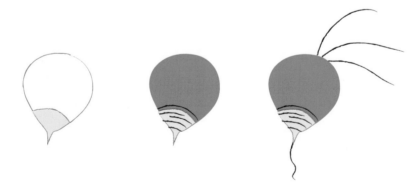

This radish is a circle with a small triangle at the bottom.

Now draw the front and back legs, and give your frog a big, fly-eating grin!

Add some bushy leaves, and a wispy root trail at the bottom, and it's done!

flying bird

Begin with an oval for the body, but leave a point at the end for the tail.
Add the wing and tail feathers.

bird in a nest

This bird's shape kind of looks like the letter "L," doesn't it?
Add a triangle beak and half an oval for the nest.

Draw two small triangles for the open beak, and add the back wing and final details.

Draw a curved line for the back of the nest, then draw the feathers and some detail lines to show the twigs in the nest.

grasshopper

Draw a circle for the head and a half-circle for the body. Then draw the legs.

ladybug

 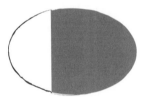 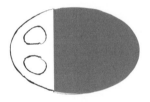

Start with an oval that is black in the front, and red in the back.

snail

 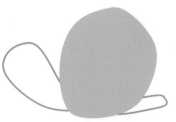

This snail's shell is a circle. Fill in the color, and then add the snail.

Add the final details, and this little green guy is ready to hop away!

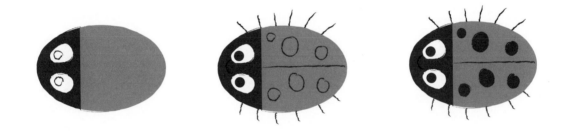

Add eyes, legs, and little black spots!

Don't forget to draw the antennae and the spiral on the shell!

dragonfly

Once you have drawn a circle for the head, add another for the body.

owl

Start with an oval for the head, and big circles for the eyes. Then add an oval for the body.

Then add a long, skinny oval for the tail, and four light blue or gray wings, and all the details.

Draw the wings and feet, and add little "U" shapes for the feathers. Hoot, hoot!

tree

Draw the fluffy, curvy lines of the tree's leaves. Then add the trunk with a rectangle.

squirrel

Start by drawing the squirrel's head, then add the body, legs and arms.

Add some branches and some roots too. Finally, add the details to make it look real!

Draw a big, bushy tail and give her a little acorn to munch on!

At the Circus

clown

All you need is a circle to begin, then add a tiny hat and a long rectangle for the body.

pierrot

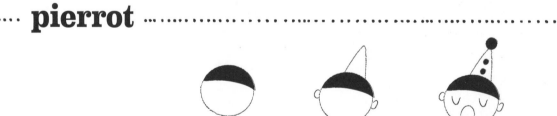

Draw a circle for the head, and add a triangle hat and rectangle body.

Step right up and witness the astonishing wonders under the big top! The ringmaster will lead you through the wonders within this tent, including a trapeze artist who defies heights, a burly strong man, a trained seal, and a few silly clowns too. You can draw everything at the circus, so let's get started!

Give your clown some big, funny shoes and wild, bushy hair. And a red nose, of course!

This sad clown's smile is upside-down, but you can still give him a fancy costume!

ringmaster

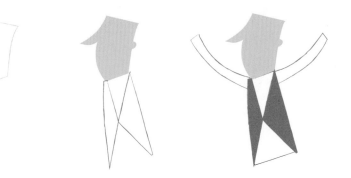

Begin with a curved rectangle for the face, and two triangles for his red coat.

acrobat

This upside-down girl starts with a simple circle for her face, and straight lines for her hair.

Draw his arms and legs, then give him a big top hat and a mustache.

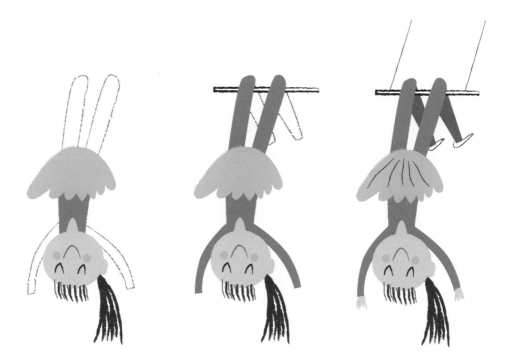

Add her fluffy pink tutu with some wavy lines, and draw her legs hanging over the trapeze. Voilà!

popcorn

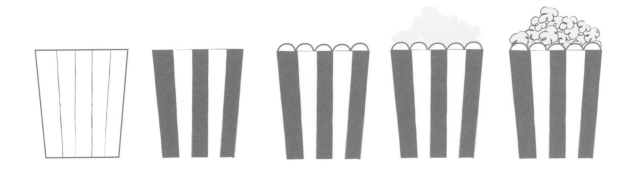

Who doesn't love some hot, buttered popcorn? Start yours with red and white rectangles, then add some wavy clusters to show all those buttery kernels!

ice cream

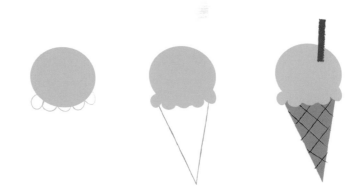

Start with a circle, then add the triangle cone and wavy lines to show the drips.

ticket

Admit one, please! Draw rectangle around the words,
then add the outline of the ticket shape and fill in.

cotton candy

One big wavy pink line will do for the main shape, then add the handle and some fluffy details!

seal with ball

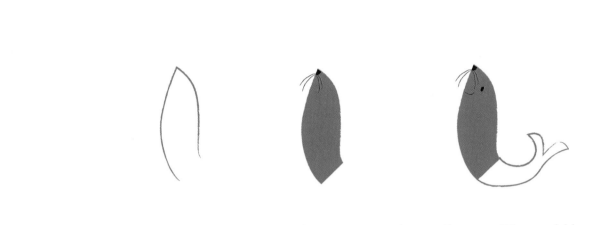

Begin with two curved lines that end in a point at the seal's nose. Then add her tail.

horse with rider

Draw a jelly bean shape for the horse's body, then add her neck, head and legs.
Use curved lines for her tail, and draw her colorful saddle and the plume on her mane.

Draw her front flippers too, then draw a big red ball for her to spin and wow the crowds!

Next draw the dancer. Begin with the shapes of her head, skirt and body,
then add the rest of the final details!

strong man

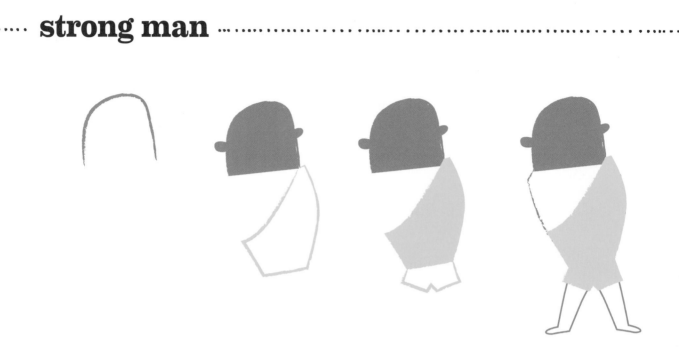

Use a half-oval for his head, then add his body and the triangular shape of his costume.

circus elephant

 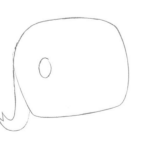  

Start with a square with rounded edges for her body,
then draw her curved trunk and the outline of her ear.

Add his arms and legs, then give him a heavy weight to lift and a big, curly mustache!

Add her legs and give her a gorgeous jewel to wear, then draw her platform too.

circus tent

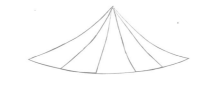

The top of the tent is a triangle, but with curved lines.
Draw the stripes, and then add two curved rectangles for the sides.

ferris wheel

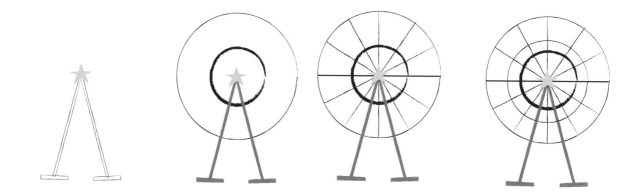

Place a star in the center, and add the two long supports. Then draw
two circles around the center, and add lines coming out from the center to the edge.

Add more stripes and the rest of the details, including a black triangle in the center to show the depth of the tent.

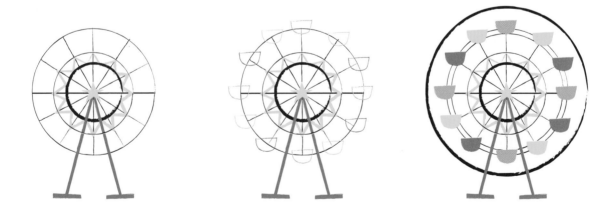

Add the seats, two more circles, and all the final details. All aboard!

TICKET
admits 1

TICKET admits 1

155

At the Show

acoustic guitar

Draw the round shape of the guitar base, then add some details.

violin

Draw the body of the violin with four half-circles, then add the neck and other details.

Lights, cameras, action! It's opening night, and we've got a quite a show to put on for you. Rockin' pop stars and their instruments, graceful dancers, mystifying magicians, elegant movie stars, and more—you'll find them all at the show. So let's get on with the show and learn to draw them all!

Now add the neck of the guitar, and all the strings and pegs.

Then draw the rest of the details, including the four strings.

horn

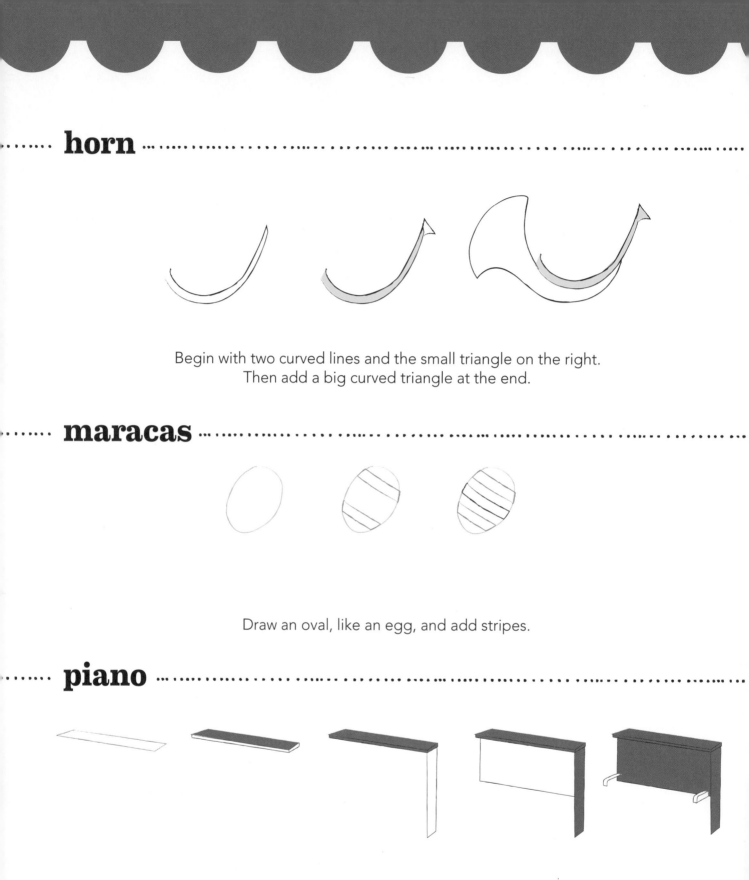

Begin with two curved lines and the small triangle on the right.
Then add a big curved triangle at the end.

maracas

Draw an oval, like an egg, and add stripes.

piano

Start at the top of the piano with a long, skinny rectangle. Then add the side and back.

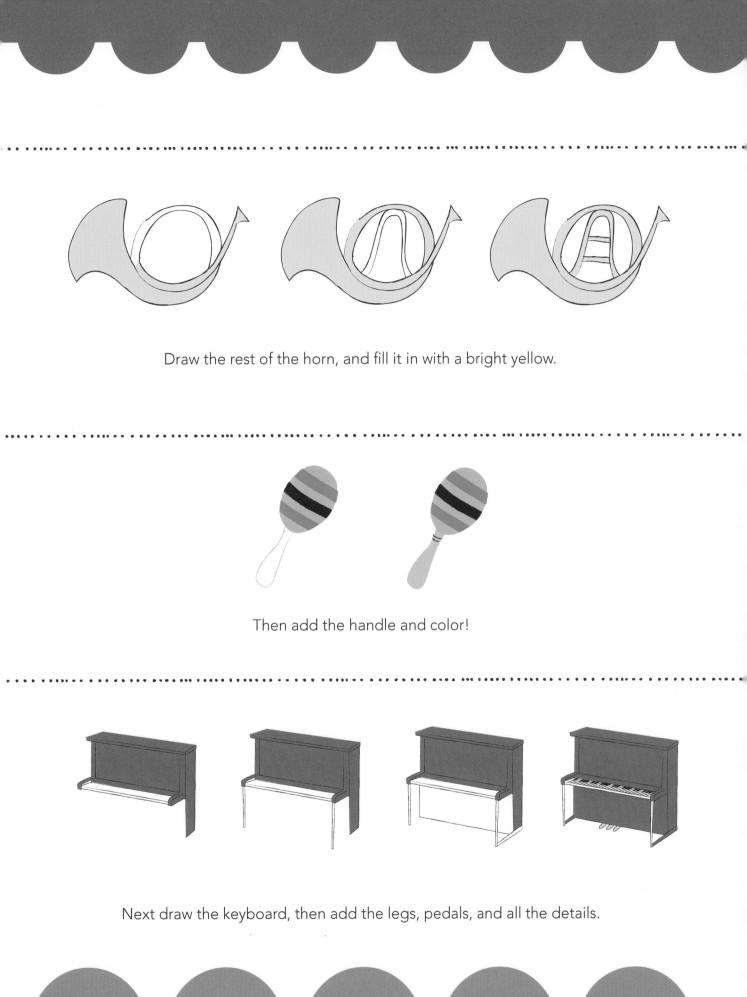

Draw the rest of the horn, and fill it in with a bright yellow.

Then add the handle and color!

Next draw the keyboard, then add the legs, pedals, and all the details.

theater masks

Each mask is like a half of an oval, with more half-ovals for the eyes and mouths.

ballet shoes

Start with two thin ovals, and draw two more ovals inside.

ballerina

Draw the dancer's face first, then add her body and fluffy tutu.

Make the sad mask dark, and add ribbons to both.

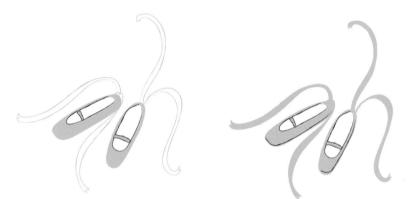

Add the straps and ties, and make them a beautiful pink!

Add her arms with graceful curved lines, then draw her legs and add her ballet shoes.

movie star

Start with her face, then add her big, round hair and the top of her dress.

film reel

Draw two ovals, one inside of the other,
then add the shapes inside the reel and curved lines for the film.

Use long, curvy lines to draw the shape of her dress, and give her long gloves and jewelry.

scene clapboard

  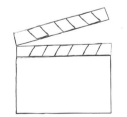 

Action! This is all straight lines and angles—even the stripes!

pop star

Start with a circle for his head, then add his spiky hair and some thin rectangles for his body.

electric guitar

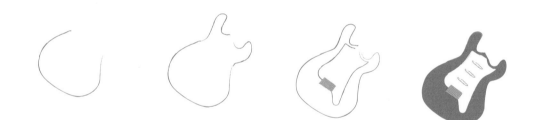

This guitar might look hard, but it's not! Just start with a curved line for the base and add some details inside.

drum set

Begin with a double circle for the bass drum, then add the ovals for the rest. Add the sides and feet.

Add his legs and draw one arm pointing up. Give him a mic too!

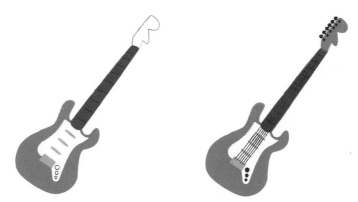

Use long straight lines for the neck of the guitar, and add the final details.

Next add the cymbals and connect everything together with the details.

magician

Draw an oval shape for his face, then add his hair and curly mustache.

magician's hat and rabbit

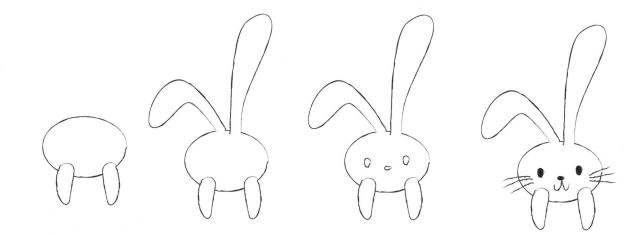

Start with an oval for his head and two more for his paws, then add his floppy ears.

Draw a rectangle for his body, and add his long, outstretched arms.
Give him a cape too!

Draw the hat around him with curved lines, and color it black.

In a Fairy Tale

····· **fairy** ··

Draw the fairy's fair face first, then add her pink dress and legs.

····· **frog prince** ···

First draw this guy's big eyes, then add his face and legs.

In the world of pretty princesses, towering castles, and fierce dragons, anything is possible! Tell a fantastic tale by learning to draw a chivalrous knight, a majestic unicorn, and an elegant mermaid. Fairy tales really do come true!

Now draw her wings and arms, and draw her a wand she can grant wishes with!

Draw a golden crown on his head, and he's ready to get kissed!

prince

Draw an oval for his face, and add his crown with three yellow triangles.

princess

This lovely princess has her head tilted slightly to the side, so you'll want to draw her face looking right.

Then draw his body and legs with rectangles, and give him a fancy suit and boots!

Give her a beautiful gown to wear using curved lines, and add long, wavy lines for her hair.
Add a crown too!

dragon

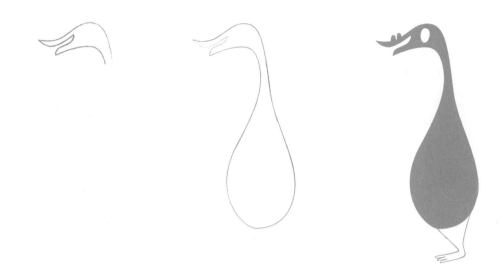

This fire-breathing dragon has a tiny head and a big, round belly!

knight

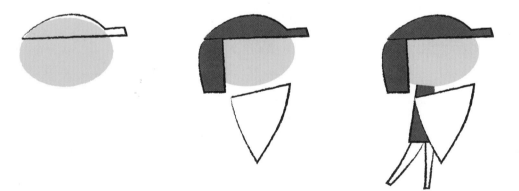

Use an oval for the knight's head, and a triangle for his shield.

Be sure to give him plenty of spiky scales and draw him belching a bit of fire.

Draw a feathery plume on top of his head and give him a sword to battle the dragon!

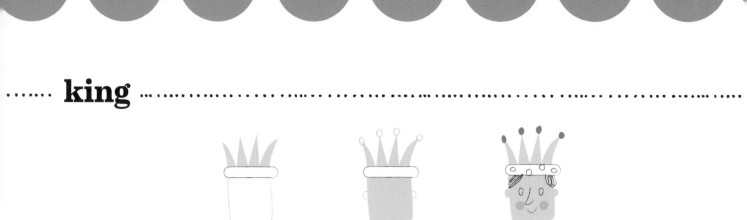

king

Place a regal crown on this king's head, with skinny triangles and dots on top.

queen

Draw the queen's head with a circle, then add her sparkling crown.

For his long cape, use a bright color and add some dots on the trim.

Draw her cape first, then add her gown and all the rest.

mermaid

Begin with an oval for her head, and then draw the shapes of her hair and body.

elf

Draw a circle for the elf's head, and a rounded triangle for his hat. Add his body and pointy ear.

Use curved lines for her tail, and add a sea star in her hair!

Give this helpful elf a big present to carry, and curly pointed shoes too!

unicorn

Draw the outline of the unicorn's head and body, then add the legs, mane and tail.

rainbow

Use a big curved line to start this rainbow, beginning with the red arch. Then work your way in.

castle

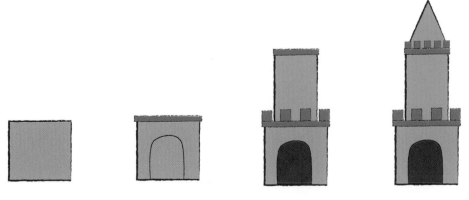

Start with a square, then add on with rectangles, triangles, and more squares.

Add the other two legs, and then add the hooves and majestic horn!

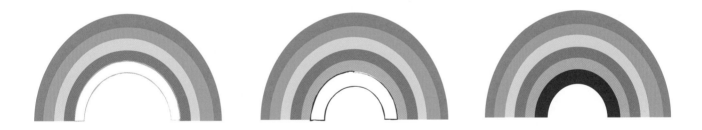

Be sure to use all the colors of the rainbow. Is there a pot of gold at the end?

Add lots of details, like windows, flags, and stones to make it look like the real thing!

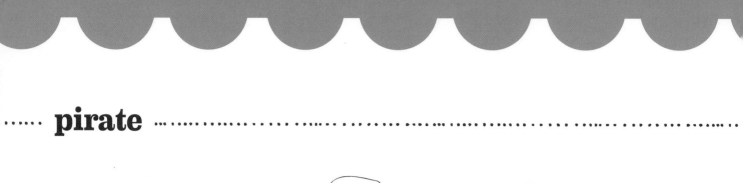

pirate

Avast, matey! Start with his head and hat, then draw his body.

pirate ship

Set sails for the rough seas in this ship! Begin with the outline of the ship and the circle windows.

Give this pirate an eye patch and a peg leg so he only needs one boot!

Draw curved rectangles for the sails, and fly a fierce flag.

184

185

Around the House

bed

Rectangles, squares, and triangles will make your bed.

wardrobe

Start with a tall rectangle, then add the curved shapes at the top and bottom, and the feet.

186

You don't have to look very far to find some of the best objects to draw! Home is where the heart is, and it's also where you can find a ton of interesting items to practice your drawing skills on. From funky furniture and fabulously colorful fruit to mom, dad, and the other members of your family—they are all easy to draw with a few strokes of your pencil!

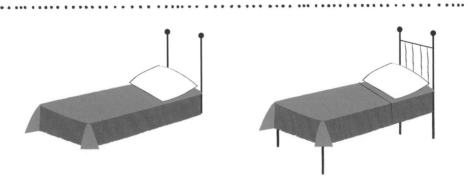

Add a colorful coverlet, and all the other details too.

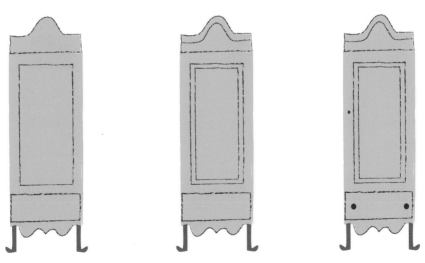

Next draw all the details, including the drawer at the bottom.

shirt

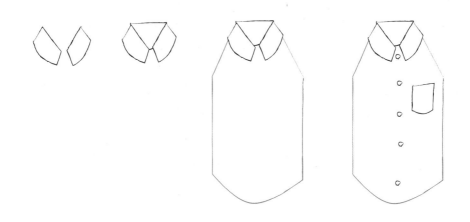

Use two curved rectangles to start the collar, then fill it out and draw the bottom of the shirt.

sock

The shape of the sock is made of two rectangles with round edges at the bottom. Add a fun pattern!

dress

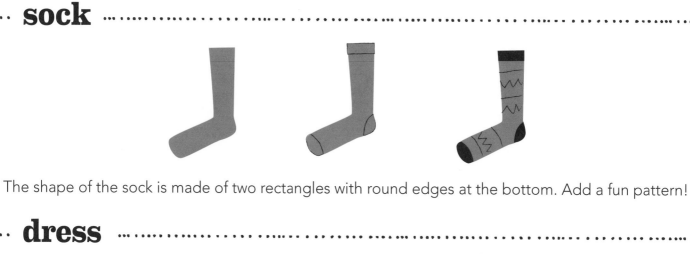

Begin with a rectangle that is wider at the top than the bottom. Then add the sleeves and skirt.

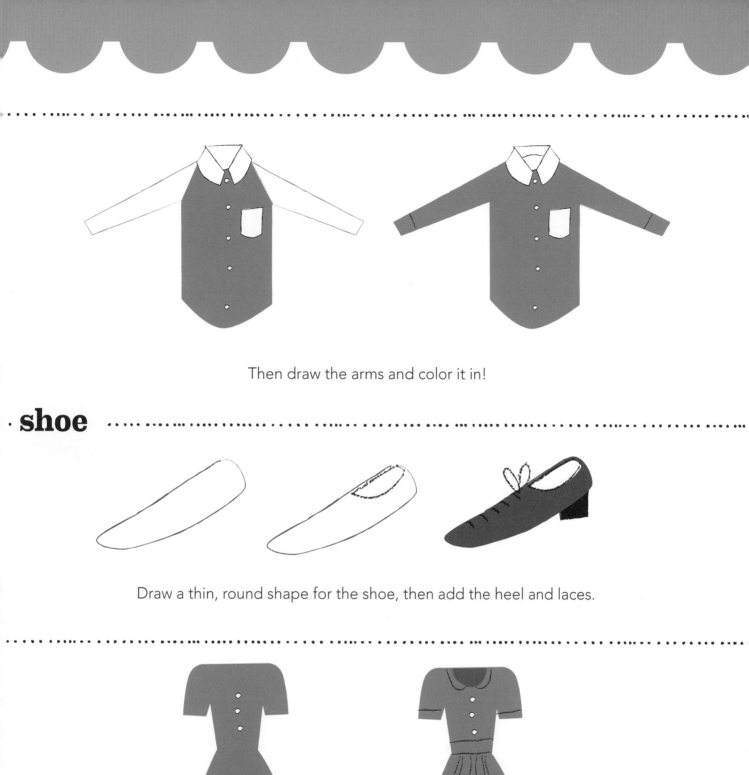

Then draw the arms and color it in!

shoe

Draw a thin, round shape for the shoe, then add the heel and laces.

Add a ruffle at the bottom, and all the other details too!

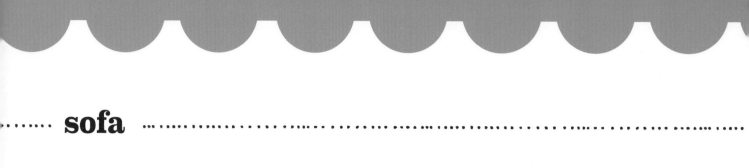

sofa

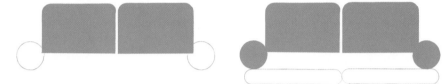

Start with two rectangles for the back, then add on the arms and fronts of the seat cushions.

TV

Have you ever noticed your TV is just a big rectangle?

clock

What time is it? Draw a big circle within a circle, then add the markers.

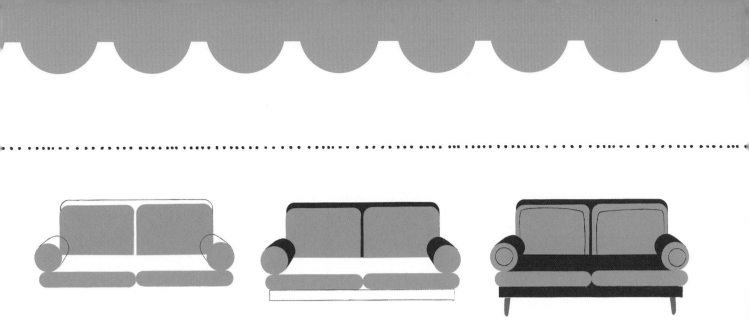

Use a darker color for the back of the couch and the cushions, so they really stand out!

You can draw the stand with a simple square and an oval.

Draw the numbers and the clock hands too.

doll

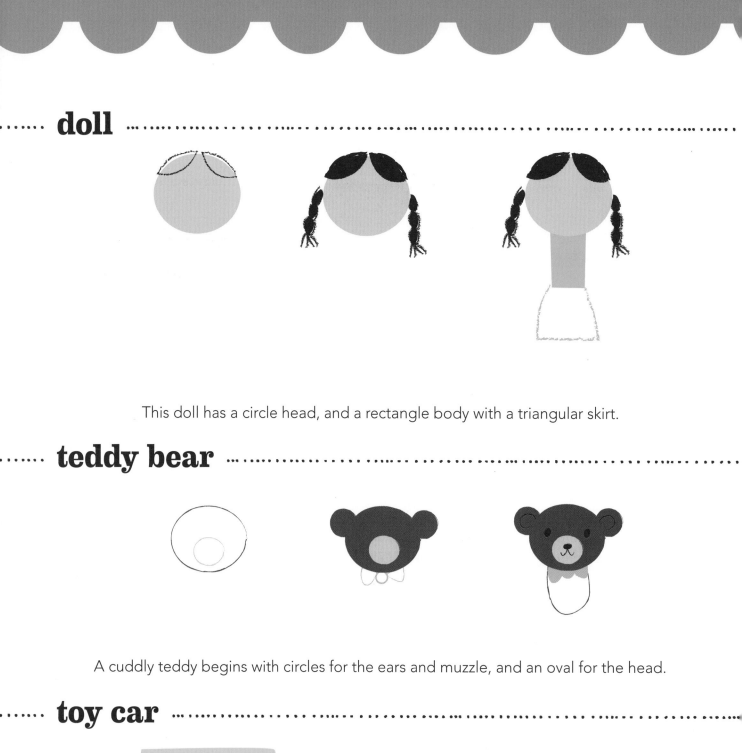

This doll has a circle head, and a rectangle body with a triangular skirt.

teddy bear

A cuddly teddy begins with circles for the ears and muzzle, and an oval for the head.

toy car

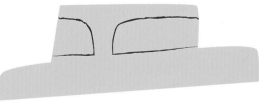

This toy car is just two rectangles stacked on top of each other. That's simple!

Give her pretty braids and a pink dress and shoes!

Add more ovals for the arms and legs, and give him a colorful bow tie.

Then draw the windows and wheels, and it's ready to zoom away!

teapot

Start with a round shape, then add the handle and spout.

cup

Draw an oval at the top, then draw a long, thin "U" shape to connect it together.

dish

Draw a large oval to start, then add a slightly smaller oval inside.

Your teapot can be fat and round or tall and skinny.

Add the handle and some color—or a pattern if you'd like!

Color that in so it's a big ring, then add two more curved lines to finish it off.

apple

Begin with the stem and leaf, then draw a big red circle underneath.

banana

A banana looks like a big smile, doesn't it? Use two big curved lines and connect the ends.

pineapple

Start with a big yellow oval, then add a green spiky top.

Add a curved line at the bottom, and a small curved line for the dimple at the top.

Add a stem and long, curved lines to show the peel.

Draw some diagonal lines going one direction, then draw a second set going the other way.

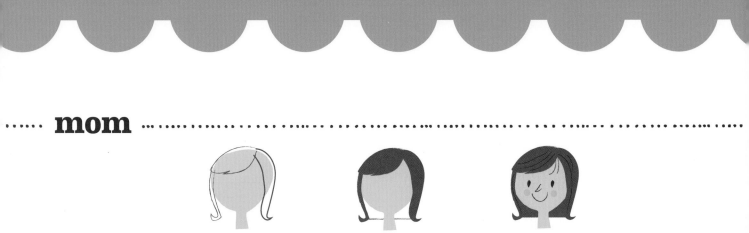

mom

Begin with a circle for her head, then add her hair and smiling face.

dad

Dad's face is longer, so use an oval for his head to start.

Give her a simple T-shirt and jeans to wear with long, thin rectangles.

Draw his sweater and pants with rectangles too. Looking good, Dad!

brother

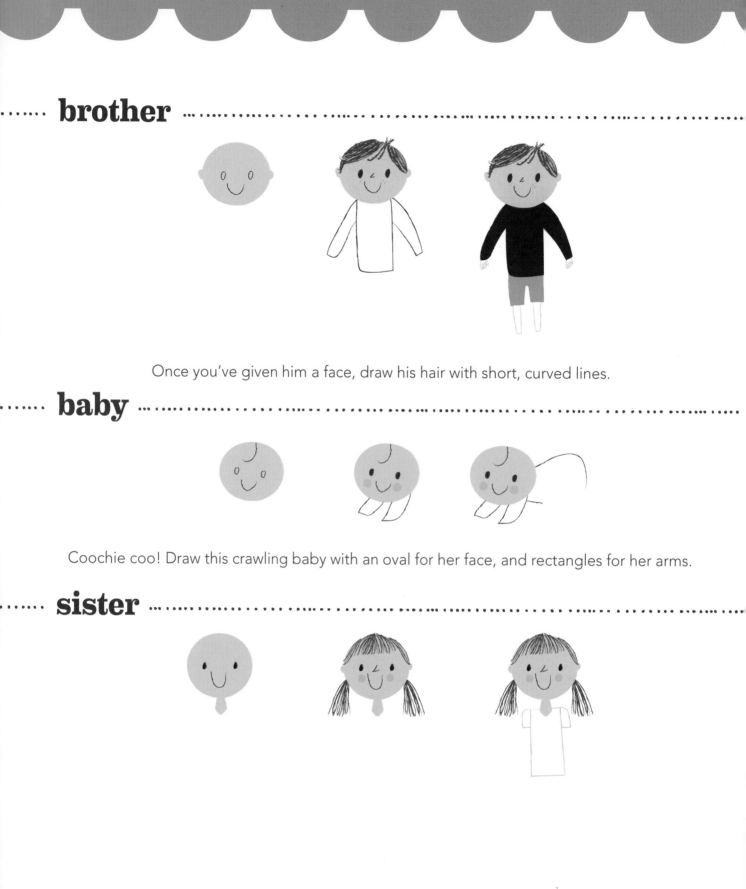

Once you've given him a face, draw his hair with short, curved lines.

baby

Coochie coo! Draw this crawling baby with an oval for her face, and rectangles for her arms.

sister

Start with her head and use short, straight, thin lines for her hair.

Now draw his shirt, shorts, and shoes with rectangles.

Draw her body with curved lines, and give this little wiggler a sweet smile too.

Give her a pretty dress to wear, and add the details of her outfit.

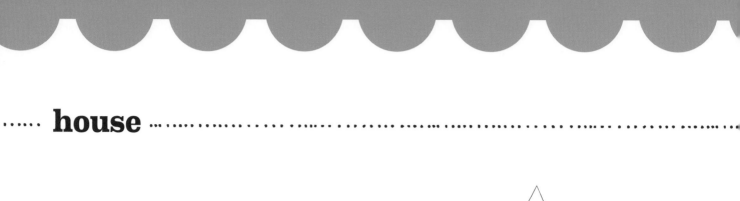

house

  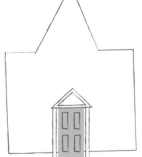

Draw the front door first, then add a triangle above it and the house's outline around it.

mailbox

Begin with a half-oval for the front, then draw the rest with straight lines and a curve at the back.

Add squares for all the windows and rectangles for the roof and shutters,
then draw the tiles on the roof.

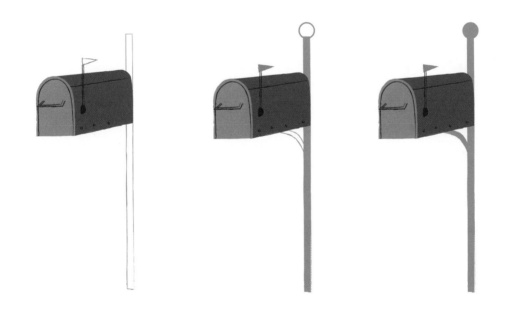

Draw straight lines for the pole, and add all the final details, including the mail flag.

S^{At}_{chool}

We're drawing this bus from the wheels up! Start with two circles and a big yellow rectangle.

backpack

Start with a rectangle for the front, then add on the rest of your pack using curved lines.

206

Today's lesson: your classroom! Jump to the head of the class by learning how to draw everything you see at school, from the yellow school bus and the books you carry to your backpack and even your teacher too. Class, let's begin!

Build your bus from there, adding the top and the windows and details. Everyone on board!

Add the straps, zippers, pockets, and all the rest!

teacher

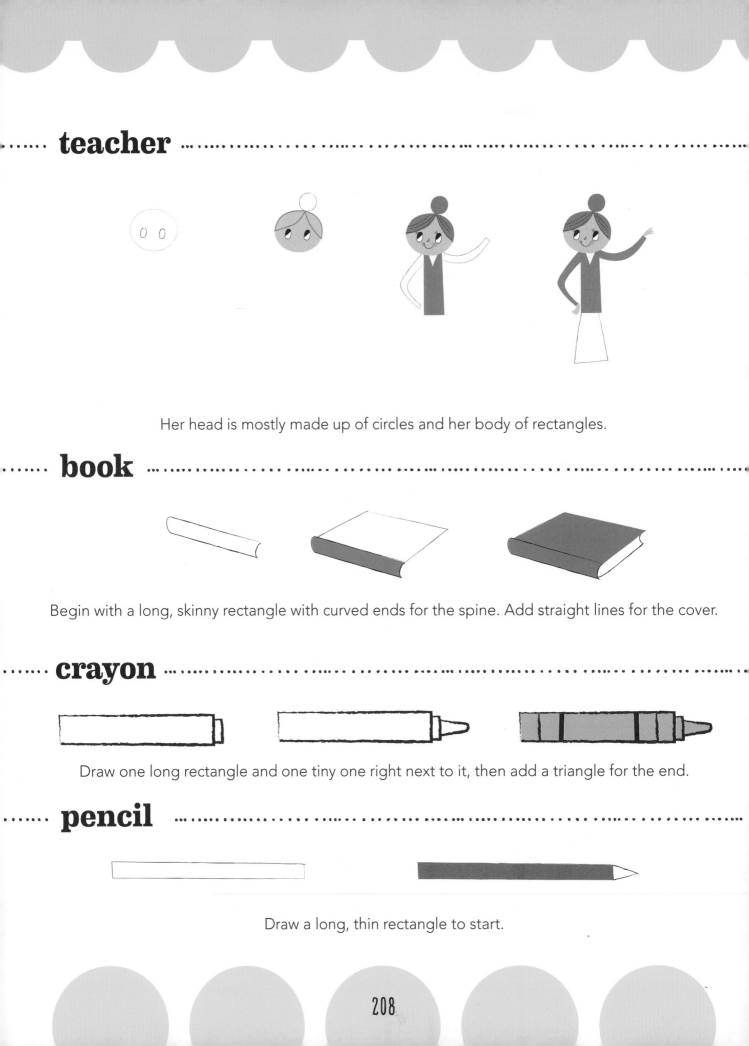

Her head is mostly made up of circles and her body of rectangles.

book

Begin with a long, skinny rectangle with curved ends for the spine. Add straight lines for the cover.

crayon

Draw one long rectangle and one tiny one right next to it, then add a triangle for the end.

pencil

Draw a long, thin rectangle to start.

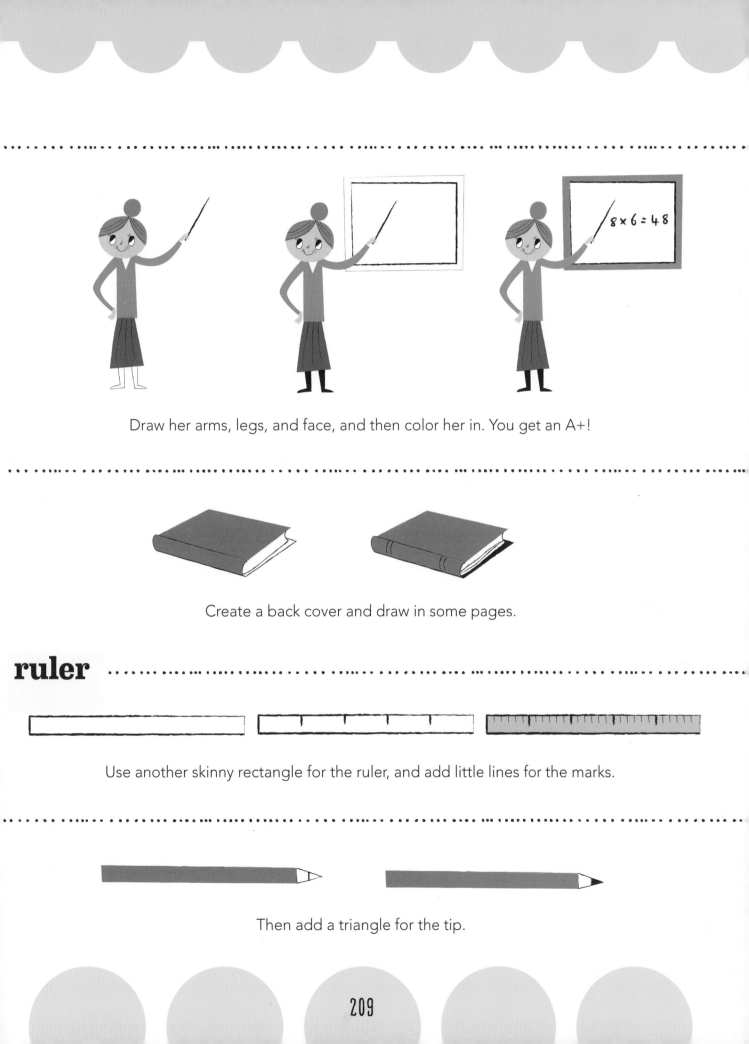

Draw her arms, legs, and face, and then color her in. You get an A+!

Create a back cover and draw in some pages.

ruler

Use another skinny rectangle for the ruler, and add little lines for the marks.

Then add a triangle for the tip.

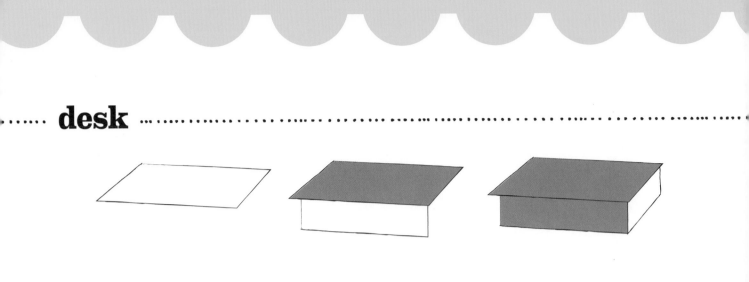

desk

For the top of the desk, use a slanted rectangle. Then add rectangles for the sides.

chair

For a simple chair, draw two rectangles for the back and seat. Connect them with four straight lines.

globe

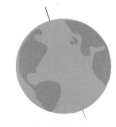

Draw a circle to start. Add the pattern. Hey, those are the continents!

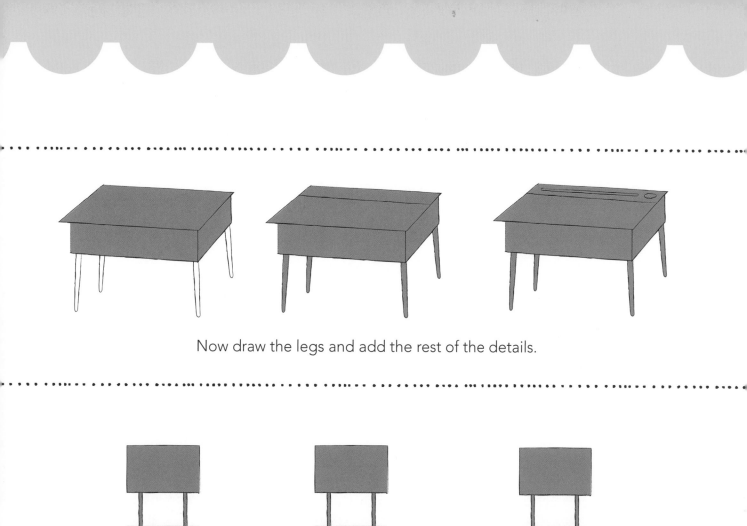

Now draw the legs and add the rest of the details.

Add four legs and the edge of the seat. This chair is brown, but yours can be any color!

Then draw the stand and add color.

schoolhouse

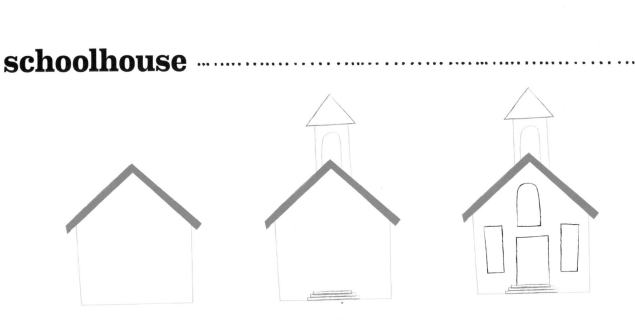

The schoolhouse is like a square with a triangle on top. Draw the bell tower too.

swing set

Draw a long, thin bar at the top, and use straight lines for the legs and swings.

slide

Draw two long, curved lines to start the slide. Use two more curved lines to draw the back side.

Then draw the doors, windows, and the school bell at the very top. Time for school!

Then draw the seats of the swings, and use bright colors to fill them in.

Next use angled lines to draw the ladder, and straight lines for the steps.

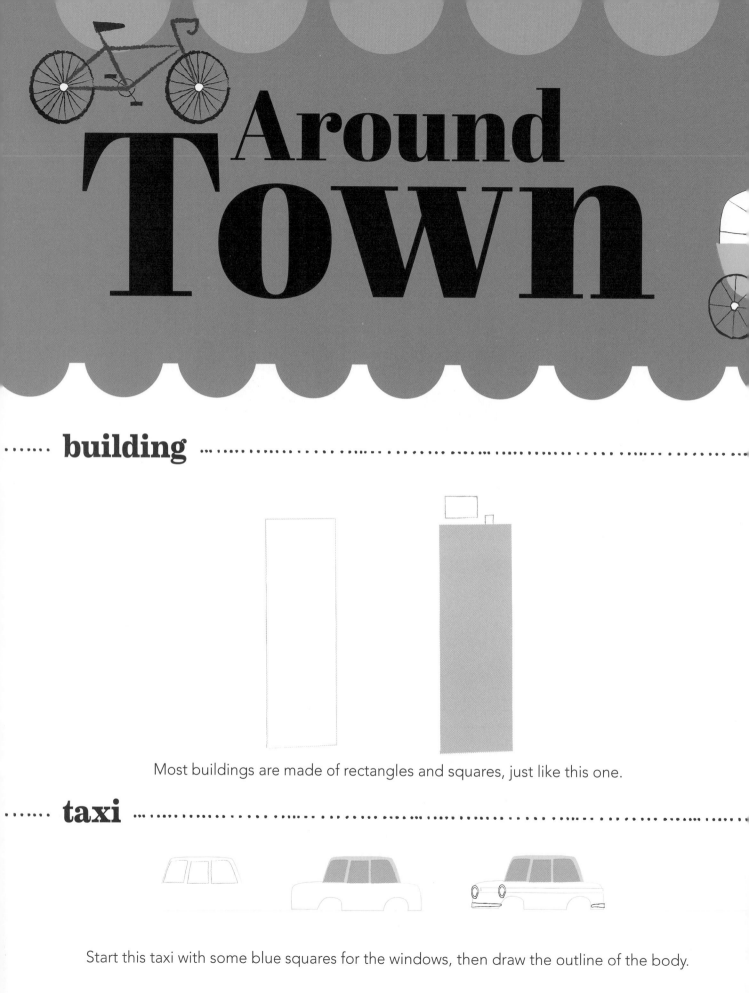

Around Town

building

Most buildings are made of rectangles and squares, just like this one.

taxi

Start this taxi with some blue squares for the windows, then draw the outline of the body.

Just outside, there's a whole world just waiting for you to draw it! The hustle and bustle of a town or city can offer plenty of perfect subjects to sketch, from tall buildings and taxi cabs to helicopters and hot air balloons. Not to mention all the interesting people to watch and draw! Grab your pencil, and let's go to town!

Draw the windows, doors, and all the details.

Add the bumper, wheels, and lights, and don't forget the checker stripes!

firefighter

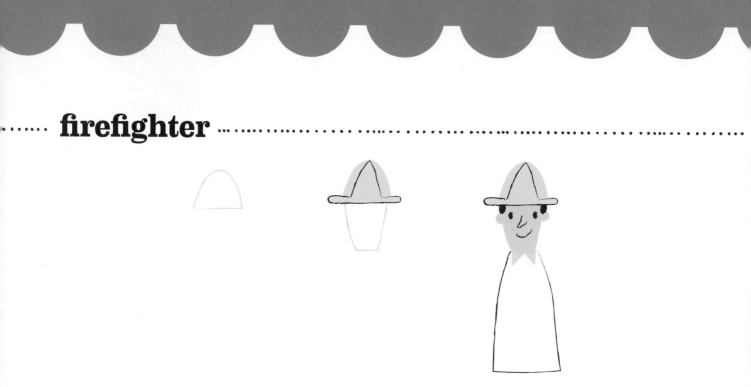

Draw this firefighter from the top down! Start with his yellow hat, then draw his face and body.

fire truck

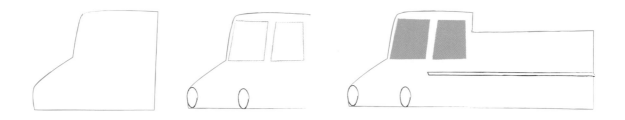

Begin with the outline of the front of the truck, then add the windows and lights.

Add his arms and legs, and be sure to give him a striped jacket too.

Next draw the rest of the truck, including the wheels, ladder, and flashing light on top!

police officer

Start with his hat first, then add his face and body.

police car

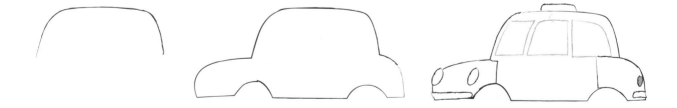

Start with the outline of the car, then you can start to add in the windows and lights.

Give him a blue uniform and add all the final details so he's ready for duty!

Draw circles and half circles for the wheels, and add a blue flashing light on top.

stroller

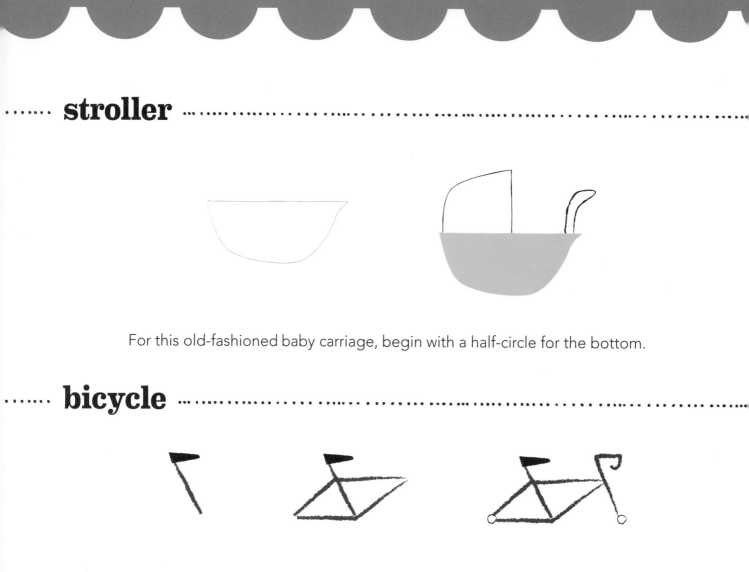

For this old-fashioned baby carriage, begin with a half-circle for the bottom.

bicycle

Start with a triangle seat and a straight line underneath. Then add a diamond shape for the frame.

motor scooter

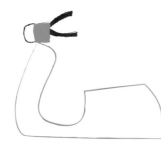

Begin by drawing the handlebars, then add the outline of the body of the scooter.

Add the top and handle, and big circle wheels. Rock-a-bye baby!

Draw a curved line for the handle bars and big circles for the wheels. Add pedals too!

Add the seat and wheels, and get ready to zip through the city!

airplane

Use curved lines to draw the nose of the plane first, then add the outline of the tail and wings.

helicopter

Begin with an oval for the helicopter, then draw the blue window and the tail.

hot air balloon

Float high in the sky in your air balloon! Draw the outline first with a curved, lightbulb shape.

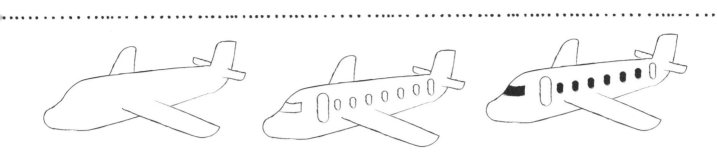

Draw all the windows with small ovals, and make them dark. Ready to take off?

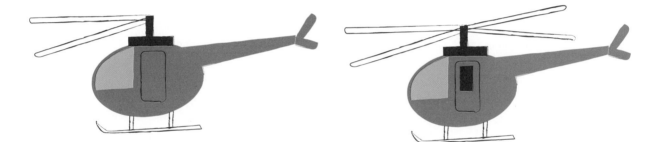

For the blades, use long, straight lines. Don't forget to draw the door too!

Add the stripes, the basket, and some colorful flags to make your balloon stand out.

ice cream truck

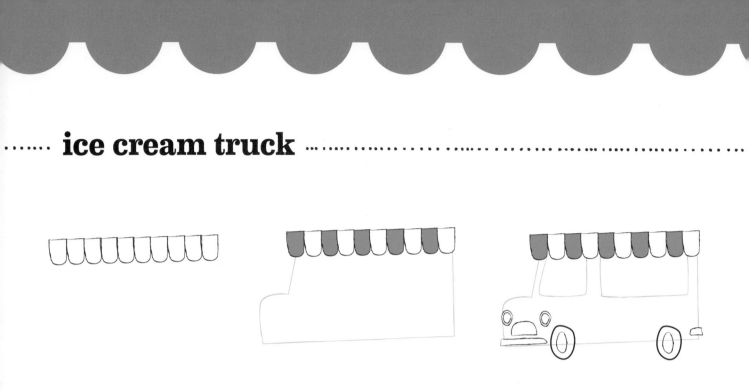

Start with a bunch of "U" shapes for the flags on the roof of this truck, then add the outline of the body.

library

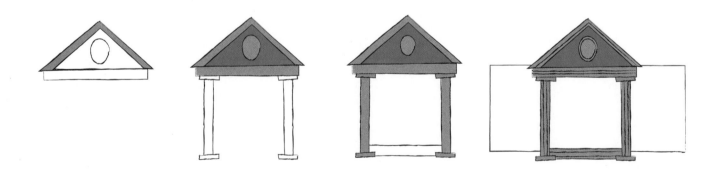

This library is mostly built of rectangles, triangles, and squares. Start with the front first.

Fill it in with a bright color, and draw a big ice cream cone on top. Let's get a cone!

Then add the big rectangles for the back, and add the tower and all the details.

228

Around the World

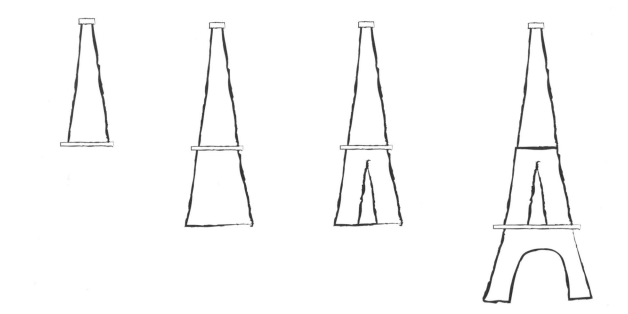

It's really a giant triangle, isn't it? Start at the top and build it from there, mostly using triangles and rectangles.

230

It's a big, wonderful world out there. From Paris to the pyramids, the tropics to the Taj Mahal, and red double-decker buses to real cowboys in the Wild West—you can draw it all! So pack a bag and grab your passport. Let's see the world!

Then add the details, one step at a time, including the X's all across the front. Voilà!

palace guard

Begin with a circle for his head and a big half-oval for his fluffy hat.

double-decker bus

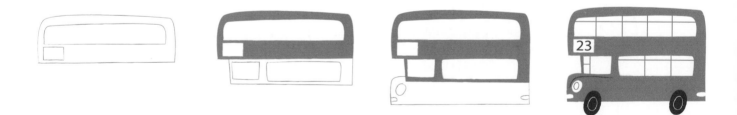

This famous red bus is made of lots of rectangles. Stack one on top of the other, and add windows. Keep adding the rest of the details, and use a bright red to fill it in!

Draw his uniform and his arm up, so he's saluting on duty!

Big Ben

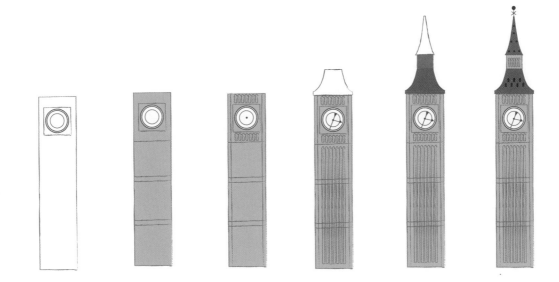

Start with a tall rectangle, with a circle in a square at the top.
Then start adding all the details, including the triangle top and the clock face.

girl with wooden shoes

Start with her face and pigtails, then add her hat and shirt.

windmill

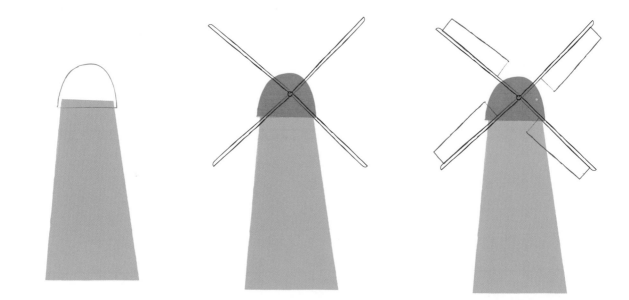

Draw a brown rectangle shape for the base and a red half-circle for the top.

Use long, curved lines for her skirt, and be sure to color her wooden clogs brown.

Then draw the blades with rectangles and straight lines. Add the windows and other details too!

matryoshka doll

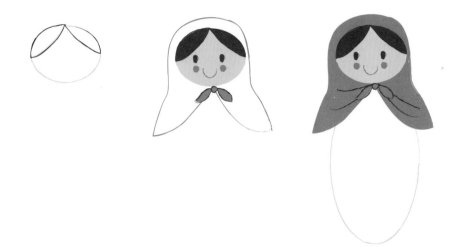

Draw an oval for her face, then draw the outline of her kerchief around it.

St. Basil's Cathedral

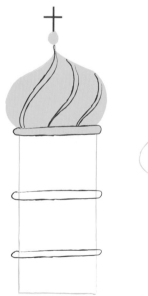

Draw the round shape of the roof, and add curved lines to show the detail.

Create the pattern on the front of the doll with lots of bright colors!

Keep looking for the shapes as you build the structure up and finish it.

Taj Mahal

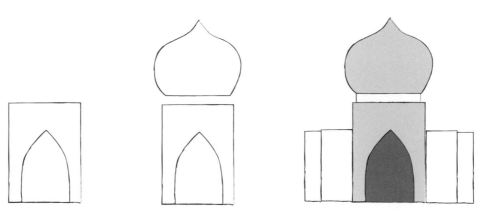

Begin with a rectangle, then add the rounded roof shape with a point on top.

girl in sari

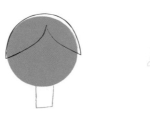

Start with a circle for her head, then add the top of her hair and start
to build the shapes of her dress.

Build out the rest, using more rectangles and rounded shapes. Use a light gray to fill it in.

Use bright colors for her sari, and give her simple sandals to wear.
Diagonal lines show off the folds of fabric!

Ancient Egyptian

Begin with a circle for the head, then add the sparkling headband and necklace.

pharaoh

Draw the outline of the headdress first, then add the stripes, and his face and beard.

pyramid

Start with a simple triangle that's just a bit slanted. Then add a second triangle on the side.

Draw the body with rectangles, and use a triangle and rectangle for the belt shape.

Take your time adding all the details so this Egyptian king really shines!

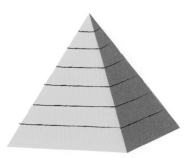 

Use angled lines to show the bricks, then use short, straight lines to finish it off.

boy with spear

Once you draw his head and chest, fill in around his necklace to keep it white.

mask

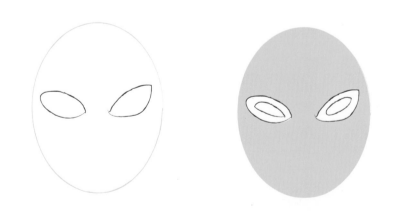

Start with an oval, and add almond-shaped eyes.

Add a bright-colored skirt, and give him a diamond-shaped spear to carry too.

Finish off the details with fun patterns. Your mask can be any color you like!

Japanese pagoda

Build this pagoda piece by piece, starting in the middle with a simple rectangle.

sushi

Make your own sushi roll, with two ovals and three lines!

Draw the base last, leaving the bottom doors white. Add windows at the top too!

lucky cat

This cat has an oval for her head, and little triangle ears.
Be sure to draw her waving paw, and give her a jar of fish to hold too!

girl in grass skirt

Give this pretty dancer a lovely flower lei and a bright flower in her hair too.

tropical flower

Start with the center of this flower, and then draw the heart-shaped petals.
Add long, curved leaves and make it a bright, tropical color.

Draw her arms outstretched, and a flowing grass skirt too. Aloha!

surfboard

Use two long, straight lines to begin, and then add two curved lines to connect them.
You can draw a crazy pattern on your surfboard, or use solid colors. Cowabunga, dude!

boy in warm coat

Draw the face first, then draw a circle around that and add the warm, thick coat.

igloo

Start with a big half-circle to build your igloo, then add a rounded rectangle to complete the front.

Give him rosy cheeks, cozy mittens, and thick boots to stay warm!

Draw straight lines across the length first, then add shorter lines in between to show all the ice bricks.

sombrero

Start with a half-oval, then add the curved bottom of the hat.

taco

Draw a half-circle and color it yellow. Then use wavy lines in brown and green to show the filling.

sugar skull

Begin with the outline of the skull, then start to add the features in black, one at a time.

Add colorful fringe and zigzag lines to decorate your sombrero. Olé!

Draw a curved line to show the back of the taco. Add whatever toppings you want!

Now add some colorful details, like loops, flowers, hearts, and other flourishes. Make it special!

251

cowboy

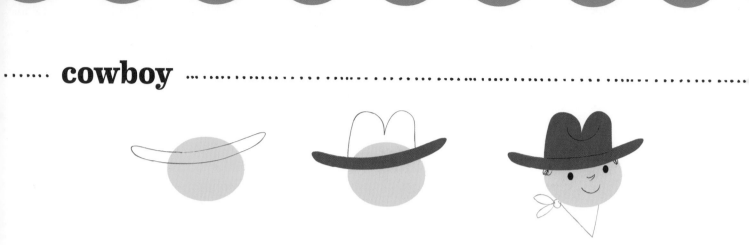

Once you've drawn his head, add his 10-gallon hat with a curvy "M" shape.

cactus

A cactus can be any shape you want! This one has two arms pointing upward.
Add a flower at the top, and little detail lines to show how prickly it is!

Give him a bandana and cowboy boots, and he's ready for a Wild West adventure!

cowboy boots

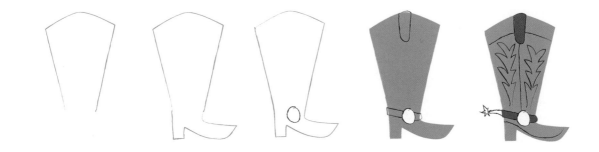

Draw the top of the boot first, then add the toe and heel.
Use zigzag lines to create a cool pattern, and add spurs and shiny decorations too.

suitcase

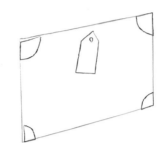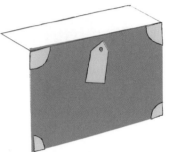

Start with a slanted rectangle, then add the top with straight lines.

map

Start with a big, blue rectangle. Then start sketching in the continents.

Draw the side, and add a handle, straps, and patches too. You're ready to go!

Fill each land mass in with a light green. Now you can travel the world!

Beyond Our World

alien

This funky alien is kind of egg-shaped! Start with an oval, then add his oozy feet and antennae.

UFO

What's that in the sky? A UFO is made of a half-circle and an oval, plus some tiny circles too.

258

What lies in the great beyond? Let's dream of intergalactic travel, and imagine you can draw anything in the universe. Planets, spaceships, aliens, and rockets— they're all waiting for you in these pages!

Your alien can be any color you want—just give him a big, goofy smile!

Give it some feet to land on, and a shiny, spinning exterior.

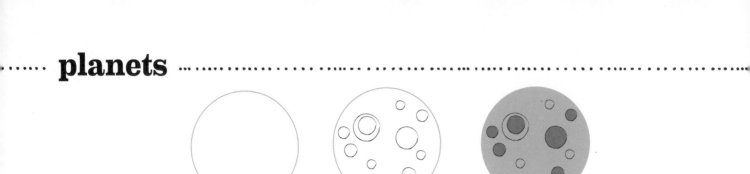

planets

Start with a big circle, then add random smaller circles to show the craters on the surface.

astronaut

Draw the astronaut's face first, then add his helmet and start his spacesuit.

rocket ship

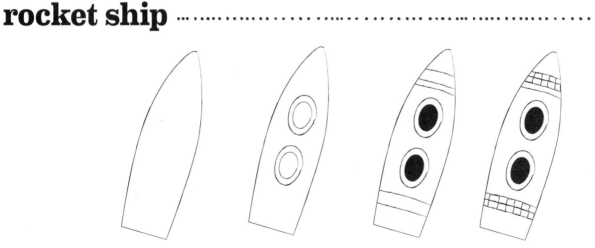

Start with the triangular shape of the rocket. Then add some ovals for the windows.

Draw stripes on this planet with lines that curve slightly up, to show how round it is.

Add his arms and legs, and all the details on his suit. We are a go for takeoff!

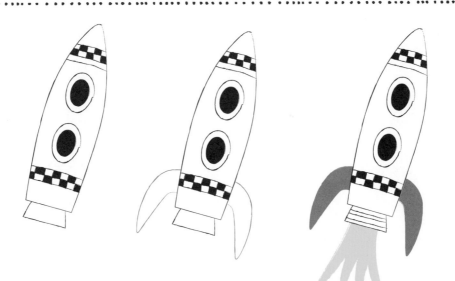

Add the checkered pattern, the tail fins, and a bright blast of flame!

brontosaurus

Begin by drawing a big oval for the body, and the small rounded shape of the head.

Prehistoric pals like these guys aren't around anymore, but that doesn't mean we can't draw them! A bashful brontosaurus, a vicious velociraptor, and of course a terrifying Tyrannosaurus rex—they're all here for your drawing enjoyment!

Draw her neck, and then add her legs and tail. She's ready to eat some plants!

pterodactyl

This prehistoric reptile had a triangle-shaped head and body.

T. rex

Start with the T. rex's rounded head, then add a big oval for his body.

Draw the wings and connect them to the body with curvy lines, like a bat's wings.

He has a big tail, but relatively tiny hands and feet. Give some ferocious spikes on his back too!

stegosaurus

Draw a big round shape for the body, and a small neck and head.

triceratops

Begin with a big oval for the body, then add the face, legs, bony neck frill, and three horns.

velociraptor

Draw the head first, then use long, curved lines for the body and tail.

Add her legs and tail, and all the bony plates along her back.

Then draw the tail and add all the final details.

Add small arms and big, powerful legs. Don't forget those sharp teeth!

Brimming with creative inspiration, how-to projects, and useful information to enrich your everyday life, Quarto Knows is a favorite destination for those pursuing their interests and passions. Visit our site and dig deeper with our books into your area of interest: Quarto Creates, Quarto Cooks, Quarto Homes, Quarto Lives, Quarto Drives, Quarto Explores, Quarto Gifts, or Quarto Kids.

© 2017 Quarto Publishing Group USA Inc.
Illustrations © Nila Aye

First Published in 2017 by Walter Foster Jr., an imprint of The Quarto Group.
6 Orchard Road, Suite 100, Lake Forest, CA 92630, USA.
T (949) 380-7510 **F** (949) 380-7575 **www.QuartoKnows.com**

All rights reserved. No part of this book may be reproduced in any form without written permission of the copyright owners. All images in this book have been reproduced with the knowledge and prior consent of the artists concerned, and no responsibility is accepted by producer, publisher, or printer for any infringement of copyright or otherwise, arising from the contents of this publication. Every effort has been made to ensure that credits accurately comply with information supplied. We apologize for any inaccuracies that may have occurred and will resolve inaccurate or missing information in a subsequent reprinting of the book.

Walter Foster Jr. titles are also available at discount for retail, wholesale, promotional, and bulk purchase. For details, contact the Special Sales Manager by email at specialsales@quarto.com or by mail at The Quarto Group, Attn: Special Sales Manager, 401 Second Avenue North, Suite 310, Minneapolis, MN 55401 USA.

ISBN: 978-1-63322-379-0

Printed in China
10 9 8 7 6 5 4 3 2

MIX
Paper from responsible sources
FSC® C101537

About Nila Aye

After graduating from her sell-out show at Central Saint Martins in 1995, Nila became a firm favorite of the London illustration scene. Nila is influenced by mid-century design and children's books from this era. She describes her work as "Retro modern with a cute twist, and a touch of humor." Nila's style is loved by adults and children alike and is popular with fans around the world.